RETRO

HERRON & MURRAY

Exclusive Books, Gifts and Stationery
Est. 1980

First published in 2016
by Herron and Murray
www.herronandmurray.com

Copyright © 2016 Herron and Murray

ISBN: 978-1-925449-09-9

All rights reserved. This publication or any part thereof may not be reproduced, stored in a retrieval system or transmitted, in any form or by any means, electronic, mechanical, photocopying, recording or otherwise, without the prior written permission of the copyright holder.

Compiled by Lorri Lynn and Peter Murray

Images: Shutterstock

The author and publisher have made every effort to ensure the information contained in this book was correct at the time of going to press and accept no responsibility for any loss, injury or inconvenience sustained by any person or organisation using this book. Some editorial may have been used from the Public Domain.

Distributed world-wide by

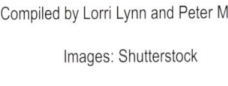

CONTENTS

4	**FASHION**	**66**	1960s	**118**	1960s
4	HAIR 1950s	**68**	1970s	**122**	1970s
8	1960s				
12	1970s	**74**	**FOOD/DINING**	**126**	**HOMES**
		74	EATING AT HOME	**126**	1950s
18	**CLOTHING**	**74**	1950s	**128**	1960s
18	1950s	**76**	1960s	**132**	1970s
22	1960s	**80**	1970s		
24	1970s			**136**	**INTERIOR DESIGN**
		82	EATING OUT	**136**	KITCHEN
30	**FOOTWEAR**	**82**	1950s	**136**	1950s
30	1950s	**86**	1960s	**138**	1960s
32	1960s	**88**	1970s	**142**	1970s
34	1970s				
		92	IN THE WORKPLACE	**144**	**LIVING AREAS**
38	**COSMETICS**	**92**	BLUE COLLAR	**144**	1950s
38	1950s	**94**	WHITE COLLAR	**146**	1960s
40	1960s	**98**	PROFESSIONAL AND	**148**	1970s
42	1970s		SERVICE INDUSTRIES		
				150	**THE LAUNDRY**
46	**ENTERTAINMENT**	**102**	**TRANSPORT**	**150**	1950s
46	FILM	**102**	THE AEROPLANE	**154**	1960s
46	1950	**102**	1950s	**156**	1970s
50	1960s	**104**	1960s		
52	1970s	**106**	1970s	**160**	**CHILDHOOD TOYS & GAMES**
				160	1950s
56	**TELEVISION**	**108**	**THE CAR**	**162**	1960s
56	1950s	**108**	1950s	**164**	1970s
58	1960s	**110**	1960s		
60	1970s	**112**	1970s	**168**	**THE PHONE**
				168	1950s
62	**RADIO**	**116**	**SHOPPING**	**170**	1960s
62	1950s	**116**	1950s	**172**	1970s

FASHION

HAIR 1950s

The world was influenced through television, cinema and advertising, and the driving force in dictating the hairstyle came from movie idols of the day. Most of those movie stars came from the United States, and they influenced the rest of the world. According to the advertising, Hollywood's leading ladies all used *Lustre- Creme Shampoo*, and if they wanted to liven up mousy coloured hair, Helena Rubenstein had the wonderful new *Colour-Tone Shampoo*. Clairol also asked the *Does She or Doesn't She?* question in promoting hair colour. For those women able to pay for the latest 1950s styles, it was a trip to the *Hair Stylist*, who generally came from London or France and could perfect the *perfect permanent* for women. How France and London managed without all of the hair stylists who ended up in so many other corners of the world is a little baffling given the claims by most of the salons at the time, but those seeking to look gorgeous cared little for such things. They wanted hair like Marilyn Monroe, Grace Kelly, Arlene Dahl and the like had, and they were prepared to pay for it.

Women's hairstyles in the 1950s were either short and bouffant or long and up-styled. At the beginning of the decade, hair was very short on the rich and famous, and as the fifties progressed, certain distinct styles began to emerge. Hats were coming off too, so hair was even more important to the average woman. Short and curly *poodle cuts* had their day, as did the *elfin cut* and the *Italian cut*. High volume hair was important, so teasing became an integral part of copying the latest styles. Toward the end of the decade, the *Beehive* was just beginning to emerge as the result of the desire for bigger hair, while the younger, Rock-and-Roll crowd favoured the more simple *pony-tail* look. In keeping the more complex hairstyles in place, aerosol hairsprays were introduced, and most of it was the equivalent to *Super Glue*. The hairstyle moved further and further away from natural looking to become enormous, flammable productions that were capable of withstanding cyclone force winds. Even Jackie Kennedy and Barbie fell victim to big hair in the late 1950s.

For the men, the early fifties weren't much of a change from the forties in terms of hairstyles. As long as it sat above the collar and *Brylcreem* was applied in the right amounts (*A little dab'll do ya*), then all was well in hair-world. That was until Elvis Presley turned up and gave men permission to be a little more creative with their hair. Sprays and setting gels helped to keep the *Rockabilly* quiffs, pompadours and slick-backs in place, and the *Duck's Tail* began to make an appearance (setting

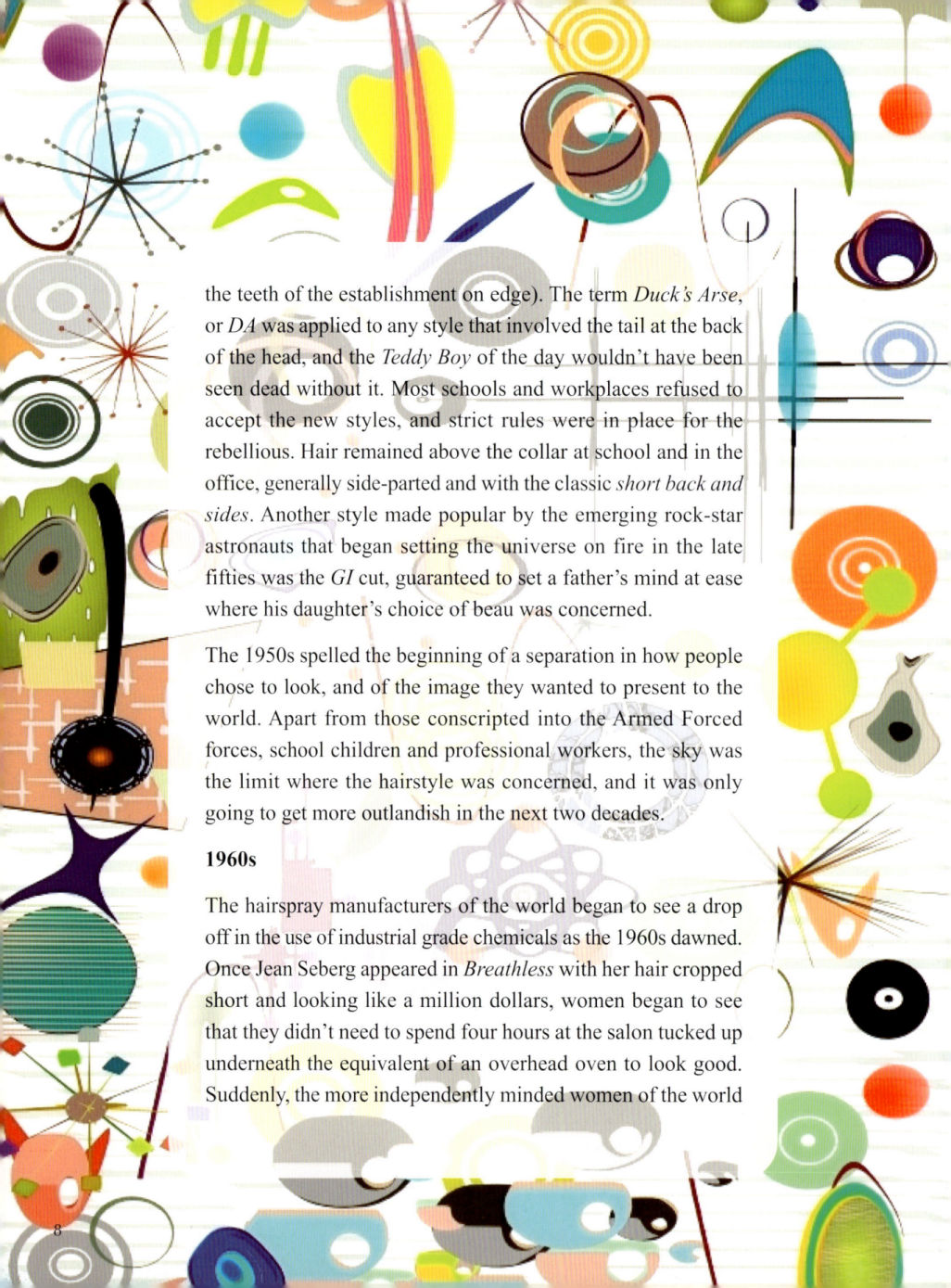

the teeth of the establishment on edge). The term *Duck's Arse*, or *DA* was applied to any style that involved the tail at the back of the head, and the *Teddy Boy* of the day wouldn't have been seen dead without it. Most schools and workplaces refused to accept the new styles, and strict rules were in place for the rebellious. Hair remained above the collar at school and in the office, generally side-parted and with the classic *short back and sides*. Another style made popular by the emerging rock-star astronauts that began setting the universe on fire in the late fifties was the *GI* cut, guaranteed to set a father's mind at ease where his daughter's choice of beau was concerned.

The 1950s spelled the beginning of a separation in how people chose to look, and of the image they wanted to present to the world. Apart from those conscripted into the Armed Forced forces, school children and professional workers, the sky was the limit where the hairstyle was concerned, and it was only going to get more outlandish in the next two decades.

1960s

The hairspray manufacturers of the world began to see a drop off in the use of industrial grade chemicals as the 1960s dawned. Once Jean Seberg appeared in *Breathless* with her hair cropped short and looking like a million dollars, women began to see that they didn't need to spend four hours at the salon tucked up underneath the equivalent of an overhead oven to look good. Suddenly, the more independently minded women of the world

went for the Seberg look. Meanwhile, the *Beehive* came into its own in the early 1960s, and it was favoured by most of the female singing stars early in the decade. Dusty Springfield and Aretha Franklin sported their new dos, ensuring that the Beehive would continue to grow in popularity with women who wanted to make a statement. It also made them about a foot taller in many cases, which made walking through doorways interesting at times. When JFK became President in 1961, his wife decided on a softer look and introduced the elegant bob and pill-box hat look for women the world over to replicate. The soft, elegant style was a winner with many women, and Jackie Kennedy became and remained a fashion leader. Toward the end of the decade, questions were being asked about the war in Vietnam, and with the protest movement that emerged from a greater social awareness came a new personality - the *hippie*. Suddenly, people were being asked to take sides, and growing hair for peace became part of the anti-war movement. Men and women alike were part of the long hair revolution as they *made love-not war*, and long locks flew about in the breeze and made a political statement.

For men in the 1960s, The Beatles began to make their mark on the music scene, and their hairstyles were part of the new face of music. Although by today's standards, their hair was short, in the day it pushed the boundaries enough to make the hairstyles popular. Later in the decade, the *hippie* culture became incredibly popular, and men's hair grew to lengths not seen since the days of Cavaliers in the early 17th century. Many

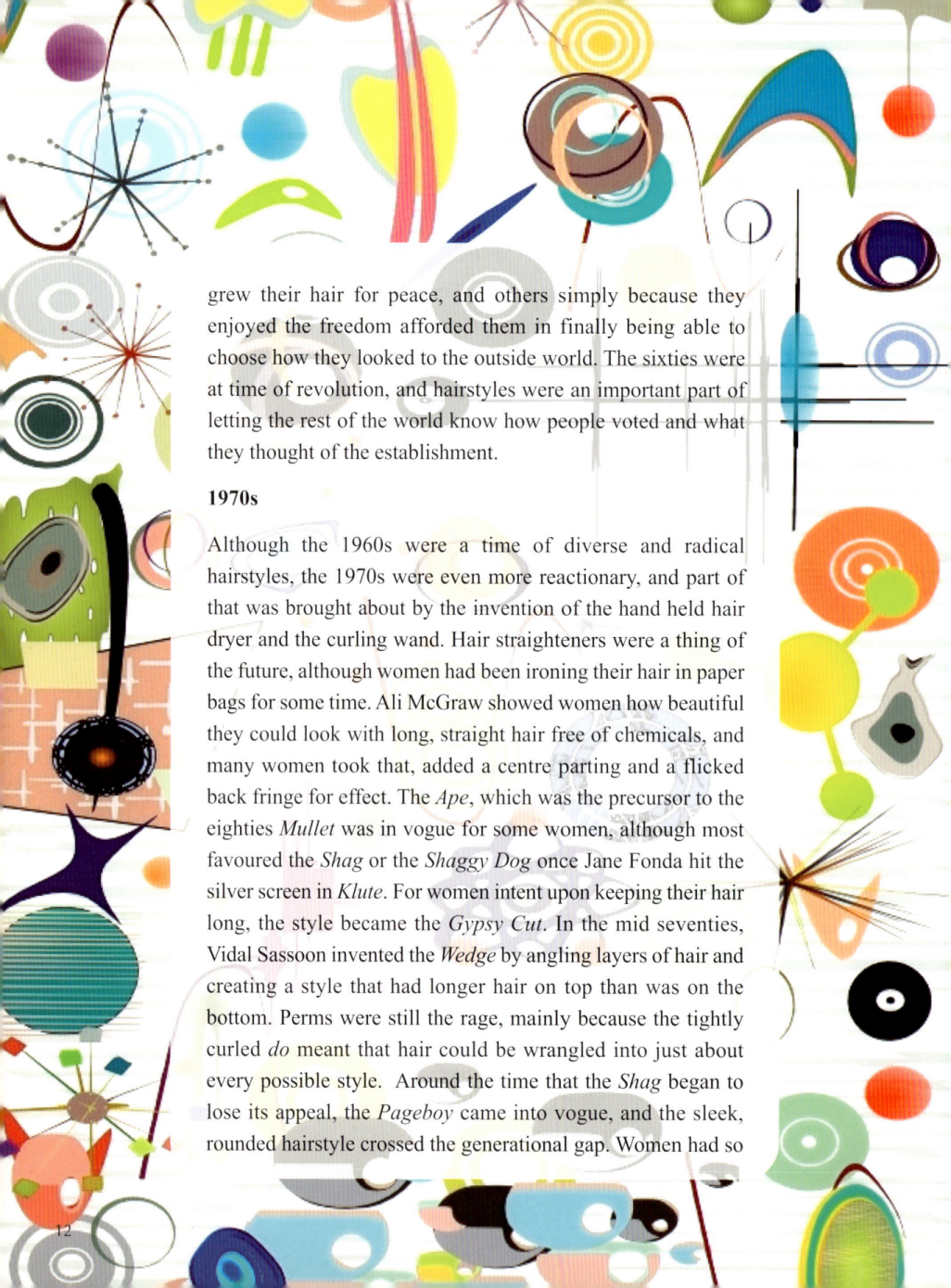

grew their hair for peace, and others simply because they enjoyed the freedom afforded them in finally being able to choose how they looked to the outside world. The sixties were at time of revolution, and hairstyles were an important part of letting the rest of the world know how people voted and what they thought of the establishment.

1970s

Although the 1960s were a time of diverse and radical hairstyles, the 1970s were even more reactionary, and part of that was brought about by the invention of the hand held hair dryer and the curling wand. Hair straighteners were a thing of the future, although women had been ironing their hair in paper bags for some time. Ali McGraw showed women how beautiful they could look with long, straight hair free of chemicals, and many women took that, added a centre parting and a flicked back fringe for effect. The *Ape*, which was the precursor to the eighties *Mullet* was in vogue for some women, although most favoured the *Shag* or the *Shaggy Dog* once Jane Fonda hit the silver screen in *Klute*. For women intent upon keeping their hair long, the style became the *Gypsy Cut*. In the mid seventies, Vidal Sassoon invented the *Wedge* by angling layers of hair and creating a style that had longer hair on top than was on the bottom. Perms were still the rage, mainly because the tightly curled *do* meant that hair could be wrangled into just about every possible style. Around the time that the *Shag* began to lose its appeal, the *Pageboy* came into vogue, and the sleek, rounded hairstyle crossed the generational gap. Women had so

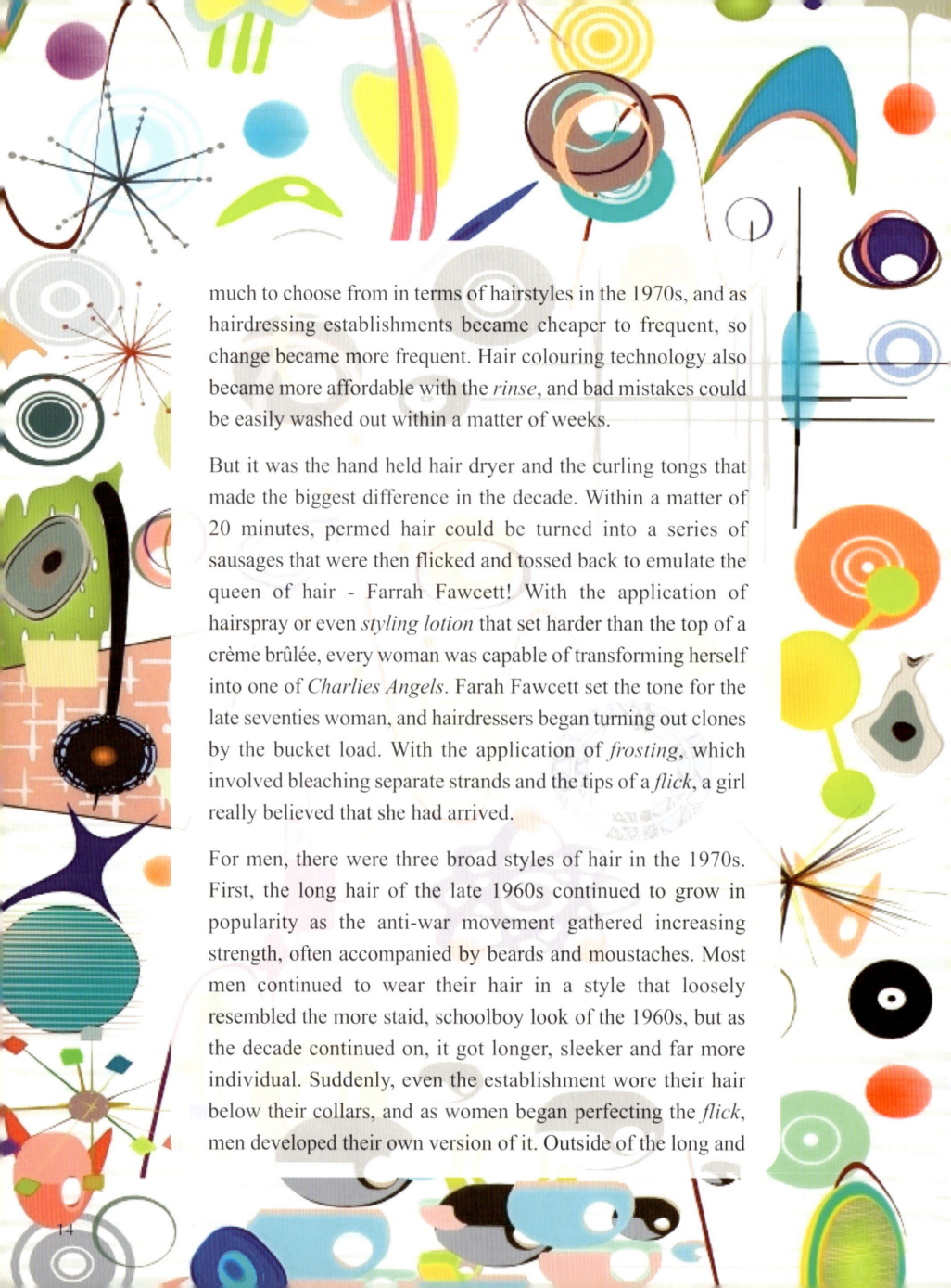

much to choose from in terms of hairstyles in the 1970s, and as hairdressing establishments became cheaper to frequent, so change became more frequent. Hair colouring technology also became more affordable with the *rinse*, and bad mistakes could be easily washed out within a matter of weeks.

But it was the hand held hair dryer and the curling tongs that made the biggest difference in the decade. Within a matter of 20 minutes, permed hair could be turned into a series of sausages that were then flicked and tossed back to emulate the queen of hair - Farrah Fawcett! With the application of hairspray or even *styling lotion* that set harder than the top of a crème brûlée, every woman was capable of transforming herself into one of *Charlies Angels*. Farah Fawcett set the tone for the late seventies woman, and hairdressers began turning out clones by the bucket load. With the application of *frosting*, which involved bleaching separate strands and the tips of a *flick*, a girl really believed that she had arrived.

For men, there were three broad styles of hair in the 1970s. First, the long hair of the late 1960s continued to grow in popularity as the anti-war movement gathered increasing strength, often accompanied by beards and moustaches. Most men continued to wear their hair in a style that loosely resembled the more staid, schoolboy look of the 1960s, but as the decade continued on, it got longer, sleeker and far more individual. Suddenly, even the establishment wore their hair below their collars, and as women began perfecting the *flick*, men developed their own version of it. Outside of the long and

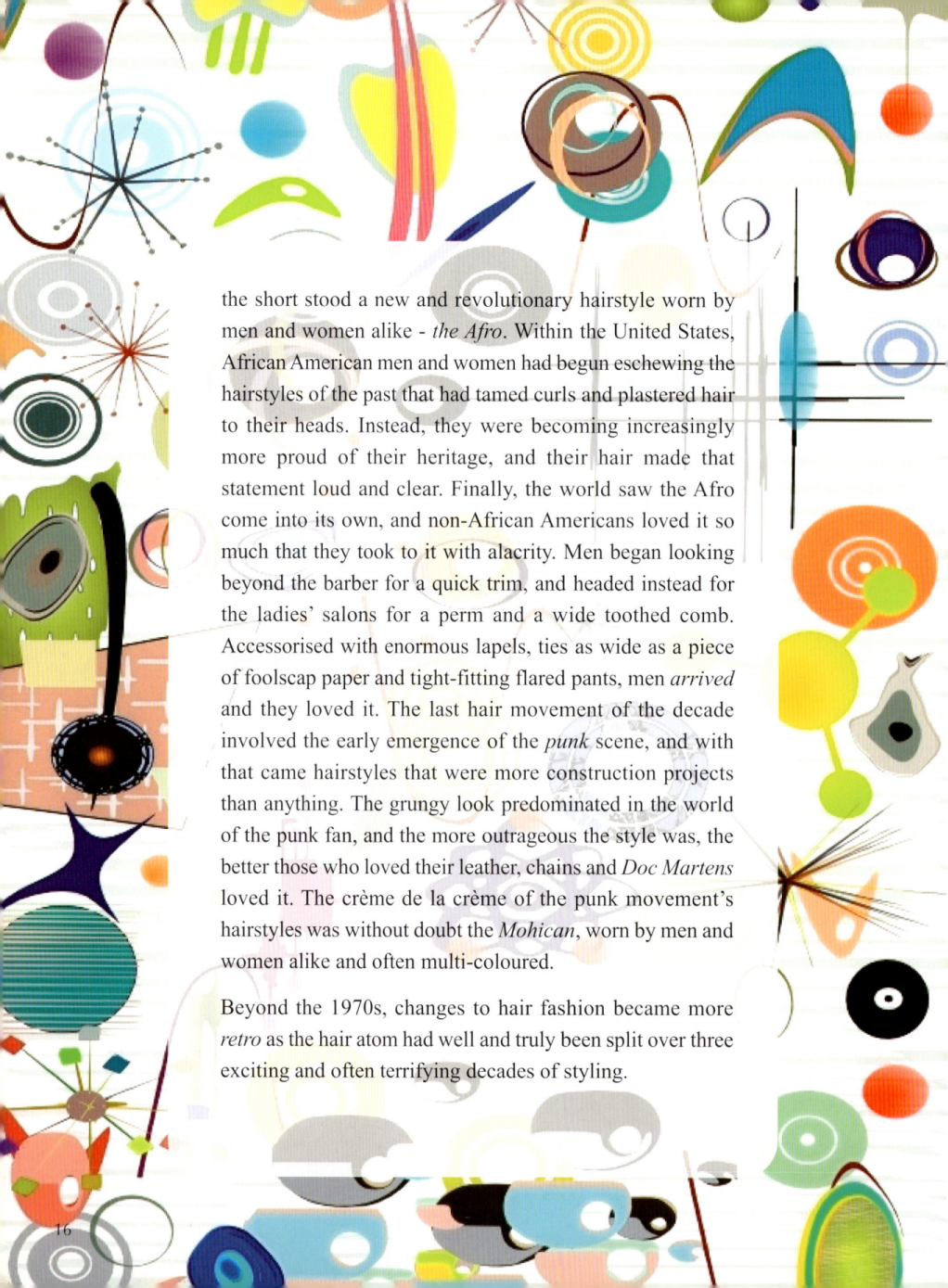

the short stood a new and revolutionary hairstyle worn by men and women alike - *the Afro*. Within the United States, African American men and women had begun eschewing the hairstyles of the past that had tamed curls and plastered hair to their heads. Instead, they were becoming increasingly more proud of their heritage, and their hair made that statement loud and clear. Finally, the world saw the Afro come into its own, and non-African Americans loved it so much that they took to it with alacrity. Men began looking beyond the barber for a quick trim, and headed instead for the ladies' salons for a perm and a wide toothed comb. Accessorised with enormous lapels, ties as wide as a piece of foolscap paper and tight-fitting flared pants, men *arrived* and they loved it. The last hair movement of the decade involved the early emergence of the *punk* scene, and with that came hairstyles that were more construction projects than anything. The grungy look predominated in the world of the punk fan, and the more outrageous the style was, the better those who loved their leather, chains and *Doc Martens* loved it. The crème de la crème of the punk movement's hairstyles was without doubt the *Mohican*, worn by men and women alike and often multi-coloured.

Beyond the 1970s, changes to hair fashion became more *retro* as the hair atom had well and truly been split over three exciting and often terrifying decades of styling.

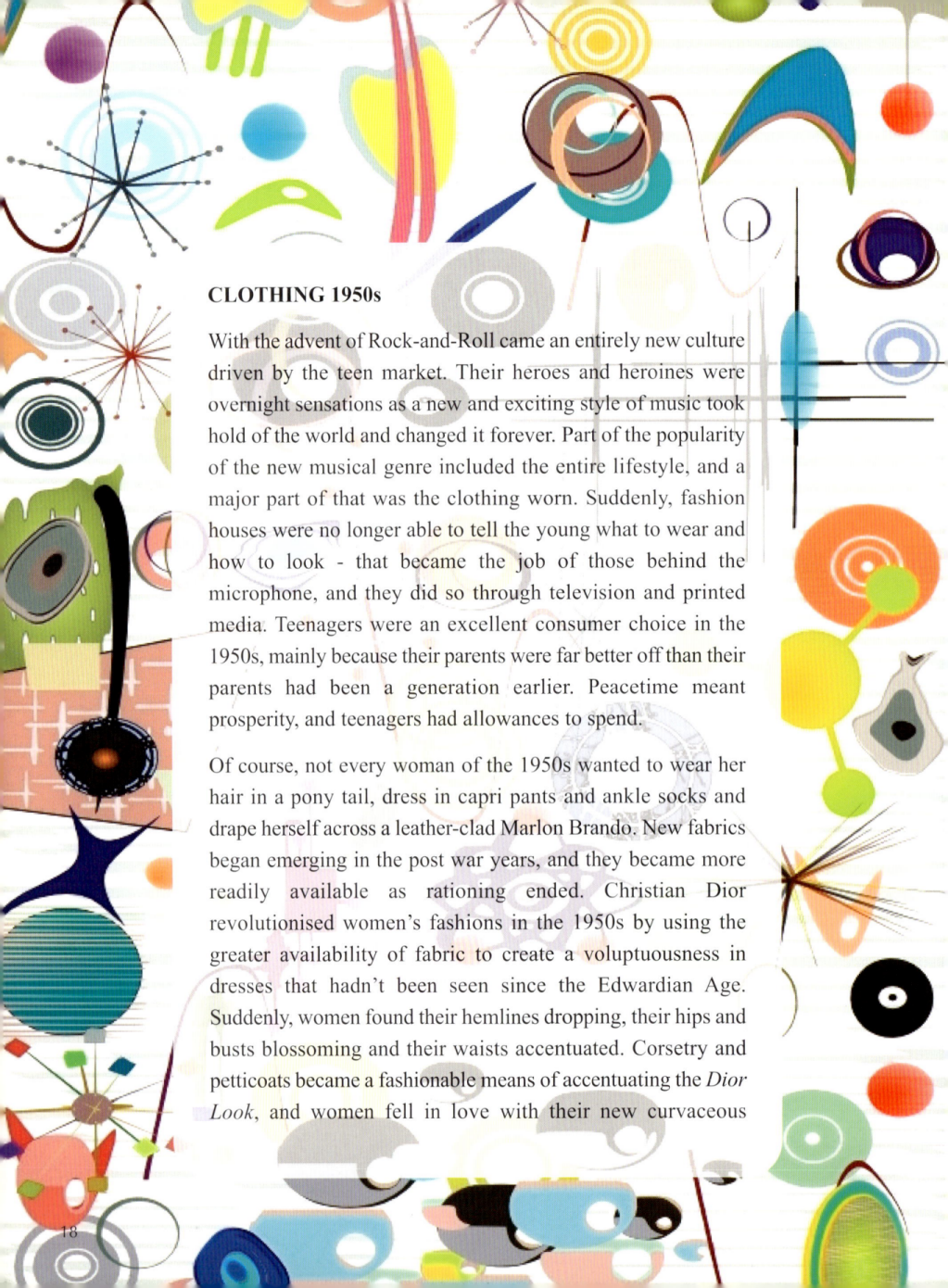

CLOTHING 1950s

With the advent of Rock-and-Roll came an entirely new culture driven by the teen market. Their heroes and heroines were overnight sensations as a new and exciting style of music took hold of the world and changed it forever. Part of the popularity of the new musical genre included the entire lifestyle, and a major part of that was the clothing worn. Suddenly, fashion houses were no longer able to tell the young what to wear and how to look - that became the job of those behind the microphone, and they did so through television and printed media. Teenagers were an excellent consumer choice in the 1950s, mainly because their parents were far better off than their parents had been a generation earlier. Peacetime meant prosperity, and teenagers had allowances to spend.

Of course, not every woman of the 1950s wanted to wear her hair in a pony tail, dress in capri pants and ankle socks and drape herself across a leather-clad Marlon Brando. New fabrics began emerging in the post war years, and they became more readily available as rationing ended. Christian Dior revolutionised women's fashions in the 1950s by using the greater availability of fabric to create a voluptuousness in dresses that hadn't been seen since the Edwardian Age. Suddenly, women found their hemlines dropping, their hips and busts blossoming and their waists accentuated. Corsetry and petticoats became a fashionable means of accentuating the *Dior Look*, and women fell in love with their new curvaceous

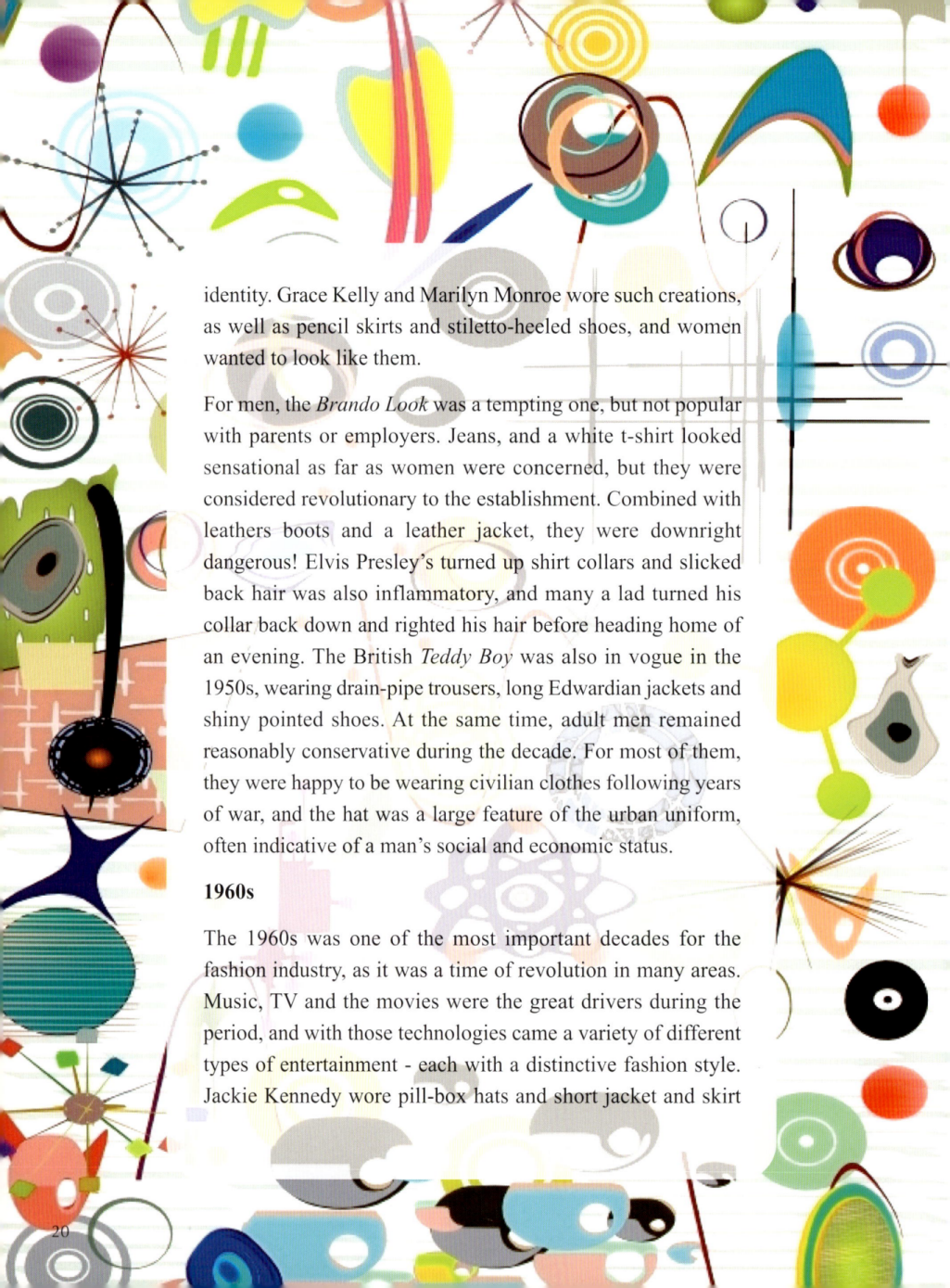

identity. Grace Kelly and Marilyn Monroe wore such creations, as well as pencil skirts and stiletto-heeled shoes, and women wanted to look like them.

For men, the *Brando Look* was a tempting one, but not popular with parents or employers. Jeans, and a white t-shirt looked sensational as far as women were concerned, but they were considered revolutionary to the establishment. Combined with leathers boots and a leather jacket, they were downright dangerous! Elvis Presley's turned up shirt collars and slicked back hair was also inflammatory, and many a lad turned his collar back down and righted his hair before heading home of an evening. The British *Teddy Boy* was also in vogue in the 1950s, wearing drain-pipe trousers, long Edwardian jackets and shiny pointed shoes. At the same time, adult men remained reasonably conservative during the decade. For most of them, they were happy to be wearing civilian clothes following years of war, and the hat was a large feature of the urban uniform, often indicative of a man's social and economic status.

1960s

The 1960s was one of the most important decades for the fashion industry, as it was a time of revolution in many areas. Music, TV and the movies were the great drivers during the period, and with those technologies came a variety of different types of entertainment - each with a distinctive fashion style. Jackie Kennedy wore pill-box hats and short jacket and skirt

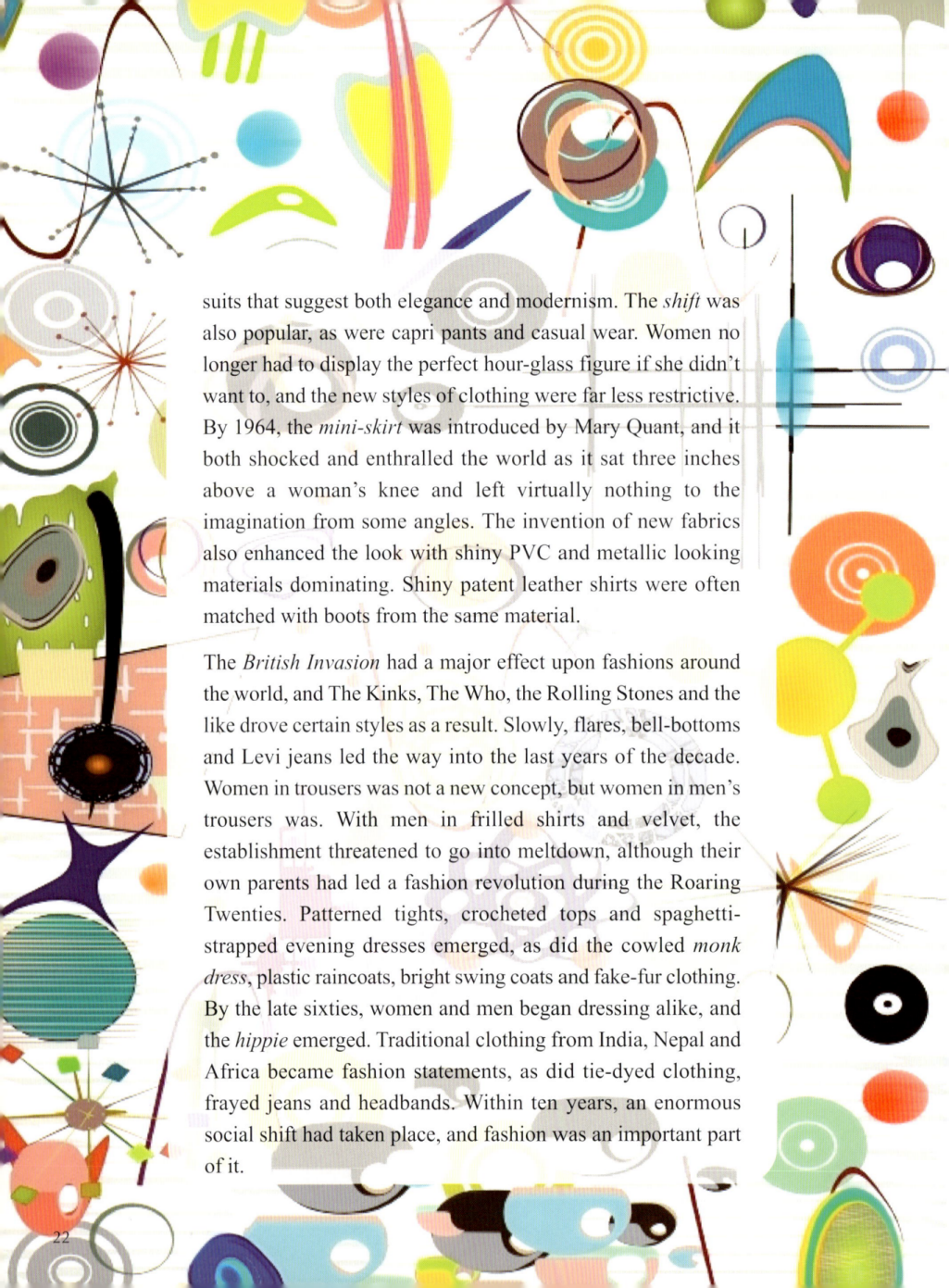

suits that suggest both elegance and modernism. The *shift* was also popular, as were capri pants and casual wear. Women no longer had to display the perfect hour-glass figure if she didn't want to, and the new styles of clothing were far less restrictive. By 1964, the *mini-skirt* was introduced by Mary Quant, and it both shocked and enthralled the world as it sat three inches above a woman's knee and left virtually nothing to the imagination from some angles. The invention of new fabrics also enhanced the look with shiny PVC and metallic looking materials dominating. Shiny patent leather shirts were often matched with boots from the same material.

The *British Invasion* had a major effect upon fashions around the world, and The Kinks, The Who, the Rolling Stones and the like drove certain styles as a result. Slowly, flares, bell-bottoms and Levi jeans led the way into the last years of the decade. Women in trousers was not a new concept, but women in men's trousers was. With men in frilled shirts and velvet, the establishment threatened to go into meltdown, although their own parents had led a fashion revolution during the Roaring Twenties. Patterned tights, crocheted tops and spaghetti-strapped evening dresses emerged, as did the cowled *monk dress*, plastic raincoats, bright swing coats and fake-fur clothing. By the late sixties, women and men began dressing alike, and the *hippie* emerged. Traditional clothing from India, Nepal and Africa became fashion statements, as did tie-dyed clothing, frayed jeans and headbands. Within ten years, an enormous social shift had taken place, and fashion was an important part of it.

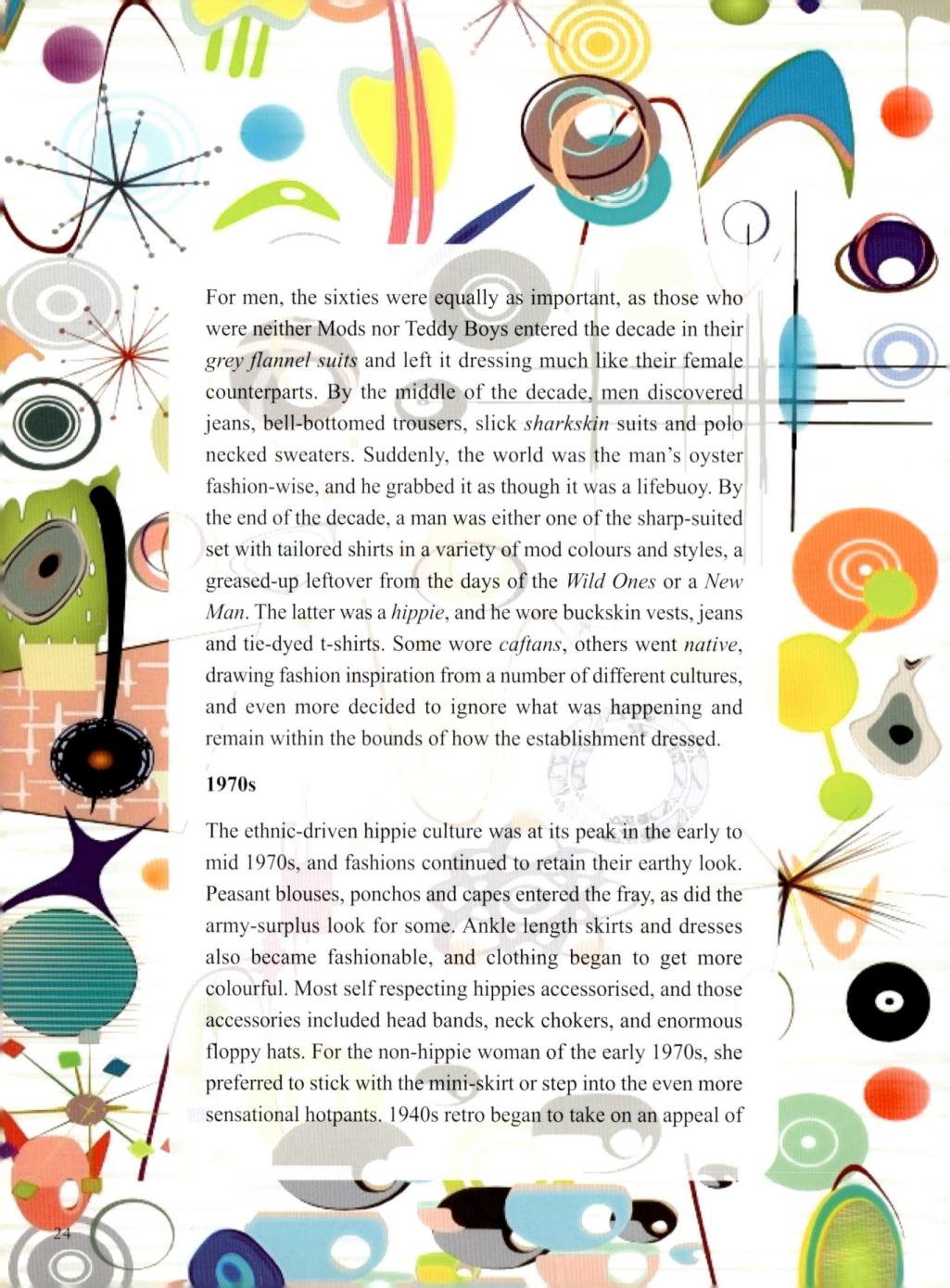

For men, the sixties were equally as important, as those who were neither Mods nor Teddy Boys entered the decade in their *grey flannel suits* and left it dressing much like their female counterparts. By the middle of the decade, men discovered jeans, bell-bottomed trousers, slick *sharkskin* suits and polo necked sweaters. Suddenly, the world was the man's oyster fashion-wise, and he grabbed it as though it was a lifebuoy. By the end of the decade, a man was either one of the sharp-suited set with tailored shirts in a variety of mod colours and styles, a greased-up leftover from the days of the *Wild Ones* or a *New Man*. The latter was a *hippie*, and he wore buckskin vests, jeans and tie-dyed t-shirts. Some wore *caftans*, others went *native*, drawing fashion inspiration from a number of different cultures, and even more decided to ignore what was happening and remain within the bounds of how the establishment dressed.

1970s

The ethnic-driven hippie culture was at its peak in the early to mid 1970s, and fashions continued to retain their earthy look. Peasant blouses, ponchos and capes entered the fray, as did the army-surplus look for some. Ankle length skirts and dresses also became fashionable, and clothing began to get more colourful. Most self respecting hippies accessorised, and those accessories included head bands, neck chokers, and enormous floppy hats. For the non-hippie woman of the early 1970s, she preferred to stick with the mini-skirt or step into the even more sensational hotpants. 1940s retro began to take on an appeal of

its own for some women, and the style eschewed the brighter colours of the hippie set, settling for the understated elegance of earth colours and pastels instead. The sweater too became a fashion item, and it morphed into sweater coats and dresses, as well as long, belted cardigans - influenced by the *Starsky and Hutch* TV series. As *Glam Rock* came into its own, so did an entire fashion scene that saw women in sequins, polyester taffeta and other gaudy fabrics that weren't everybody's cup of tea.

For women, the t-shirt came out from underneath to be a fashion garment in its own right, and even the blouses and tops of the early decade became more fitted by the middle of the seventies. The hippie look soon disappeared, replaced by jeans, sweaters, peasant blouses or shirts with large flowing sleeves. Pantsuits soon arrived, often in synthetic satins, and by the end of the decade, clothing was baggy. Women with good figures hated the advent of billowy clothing, and women with larger figures felt twice their size, but this was compensated by the emergence of sensational new fabrics that sparkled and shone. The disco look was also big at that point in time, and a lot of the fashion was a combination of old and new created in shiny new fabric and accompanied by lip gloss and hairspray. Thankfully, the period was a short-lived one, and by the end of the decade, fitted clothing, enormous shoulder pads and an all-over *triangular* look began to replace it.

Men headed into the seventies either still wearing hippie clothing or inspired to embrace a new and emerging look that generally involved beards and enormous side-burns. Sports jackets, chunky sweaters and cardigans were suddenly fashionable, as were t-shirts and flared jeans. Denim jackets soon accompanied the jeans, as did necklaces and mood rings for the truly adventurous. Nehru jackets were also fashionable and a favourite for some men, which was generally a well chosen accompaniment to the more streamlined European look. The *Safari Suit* was also a winner among men, and when worn with the new tight fitting, poly cotton shirt, it was an absolute winner in some circles. By the end of the decade, men had tried just about every style of fashion, and they came through it far more informed about choices. Many ended the seventies in disco style, wearing the tightest of flared trousers, equally tight-fitting shirts with enormous collars, suit jackets, necklaces, bracelets and platform shoes. The *punk* movement was also upon the world, and men only had to wear ripped jeans or tight leather pants, leather jackets, safety pins in the cheek and *Doc Martens* on the feet to be considered a Punk.

For both sexes, the seventies were a time of continual change in fashion, and much of what was worn was dictated by the social circles in which a person moved. It might not have been pretty at certain points of the decade, but it was definitely interesting and it gave both men and women the opportunity to experiment with fashion and dictate the outside world's perception of them.

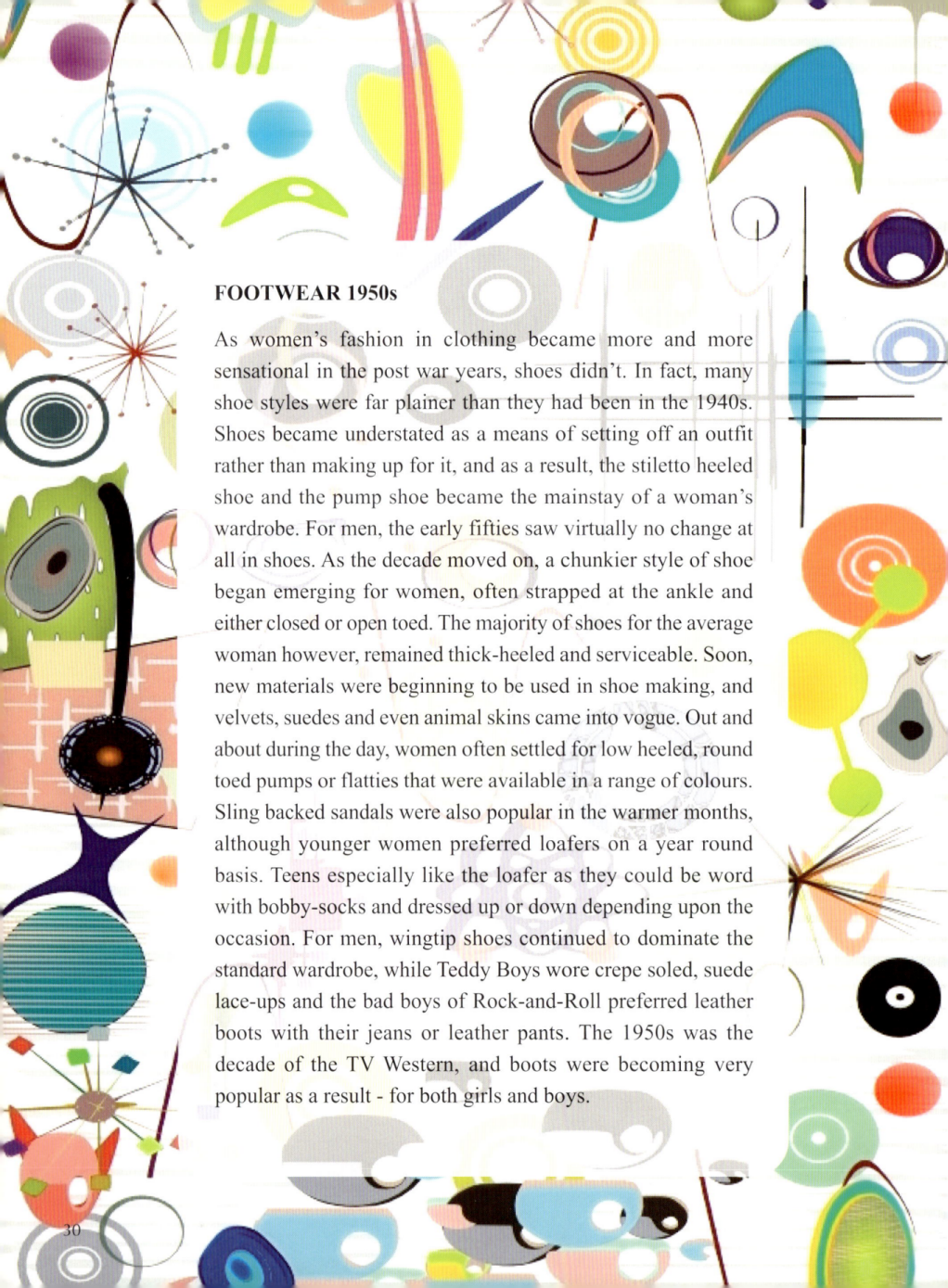

FOOTWEAR 1950s

As women's fashion in clothing became more and more sensational in the post war years, shoes didn't. In fact, many shoe styles were far plainer than they had been in the 1940s. Shoes became understated as a means of setting off an outfit rather than making up for it, and as a result, the stiletto heeled shoe and the pump shoe became the mainstay of a woman's wardrobe. For men, the early fifties saw virtually no change at all in shoes. As the decade moved on, a chunkier style of shoe began emerging for women, often strapped at the ankle and either closed or open toed. The majority of shoes for the average woman however, remained thick-heeled and serviceable. Soon, new materials were beginning to be used in shoe making, and velvets, suedes and even animal skins came into vogue. Out and about during the day, women often settled for low heeled, round toed pumps or flatties that were available in a range of colours. Sling backed sandals were also popular in the warmer months, although younger women preferred loafers on a year round basis. Teens especially like the loafer as they could be word with bobby-socks and dressed up or down depending upon the occasion. For men, wingtip shoes continued to dominate the standard wardrobe, while Teddy Boys wore crepe soled, suede lace-ups and the bad boys of Rock-and-Roll preferred leather boots with their jeans or leather pants. The 1950s was the decade of the TV Western, and boots were becoming very popular as a result - for both girls and boys.

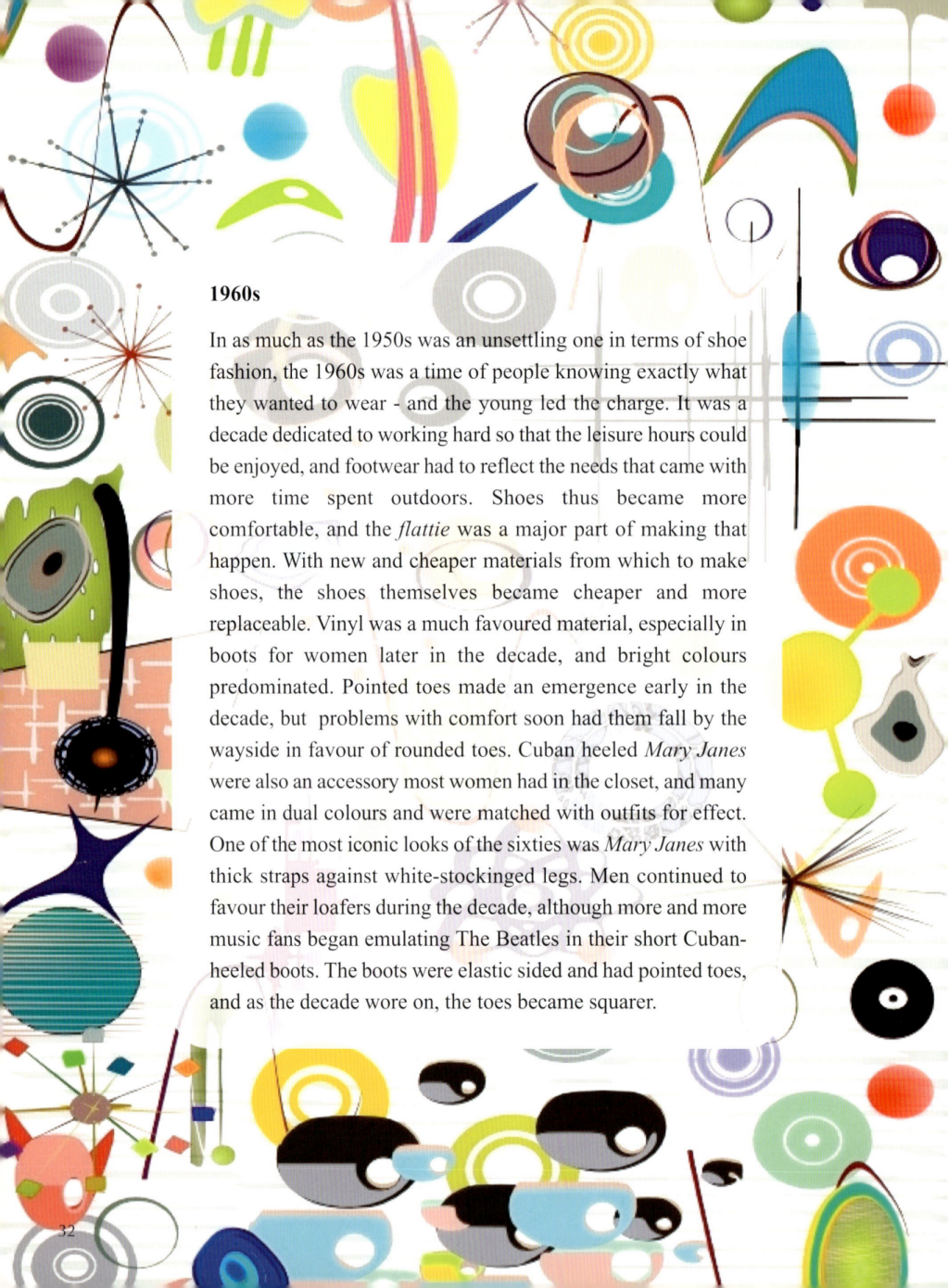

1960s

In as much as the 1950s was an unsettling one in terms of shoe fashion, the 1960s was a time of people knowing exactly what they wanted to wear - and the young led the charge. It was a decade dedicated to working hard so that the leisure hours could be enjoyed, and footwear had to reflect the needs that came with more time spent outdoors. Shoes thus became more comfortable, and the *flattie* was a major part of making that happen. With new and cheaper materials from which to make shoes, the shoes themselves became cheaper and more replaceable. Vinyl was a much favoured material, especially in boots for women later in the decade, and bright colours predominated. Pointed toes made an emergence early in the decade, but problems with comfort soon had them fall by the wayside in favour of rounded toes. Cuban heeled *Mary Janes* were also an accessory most women had in the closet, and many came in dual colours and were matched with outfits for effect. One of the most iconic looks of the sixties was *Mary Janes* with thick straps against white-stockinged legs. Men continued to favour their loafers during the decade, although more and more music fans began emulating The Beatles in their short Cuban-heeled boots. The boots were elastic sided and had pointed toes, and as the decade wore on, the toes became squarer.

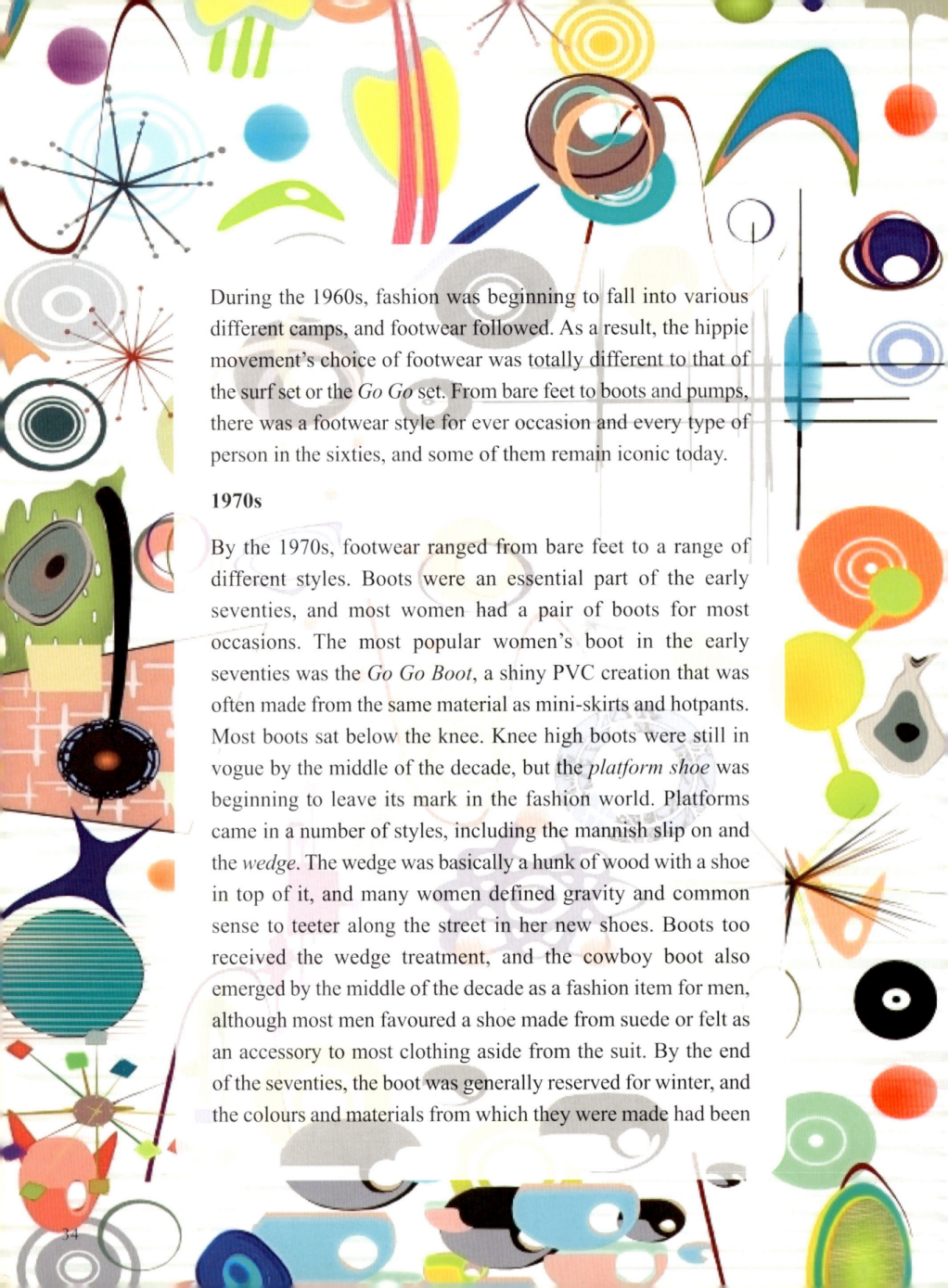

During the 1960s, fashion was beginning to fall into various different camps, and footwear followed. As a result, the hippie movement's choice of footwear was totally different to that of the surf set or the *Go Go* set. From bare feet to boots and pumps, there was a footwear style for ever occasion and every type of person in the sixties, and some of them remain iconic today.

1970s

By the 1970s, footwear ranged from bare feet to a range of different styles. Boots were an essential part of the early seventies, and most women had a pair of boots for most occasions. The most popular women's boot in the early seventies was the *Go Go Boot*, a shiny PVC creation that was often made from the same material as mini-skirts and hotpants. Most boots sat below the knee. Knee high boots were still in vogue by the middle of the decade, but the *platform shoe* was beginning to leave its mark in the fashion world. Platforms came in a number of styles, including the mannish slip on and the *wedge*. The wedge was basically a hunk of wood with a shoe in top of it, and many women defined gravity and common sense to teeter along the street in her new shoes. Boots too received the wedge treatment, and the cowboy boot also emerged by the middle of the decade as a fashion item for men, although most men favoured a shoe made from suede or felt as an accessory to most clothing aside from the suit. By the end of the seventies, the boot was generally reserved for winter, and the colours and materials from which they were made had been

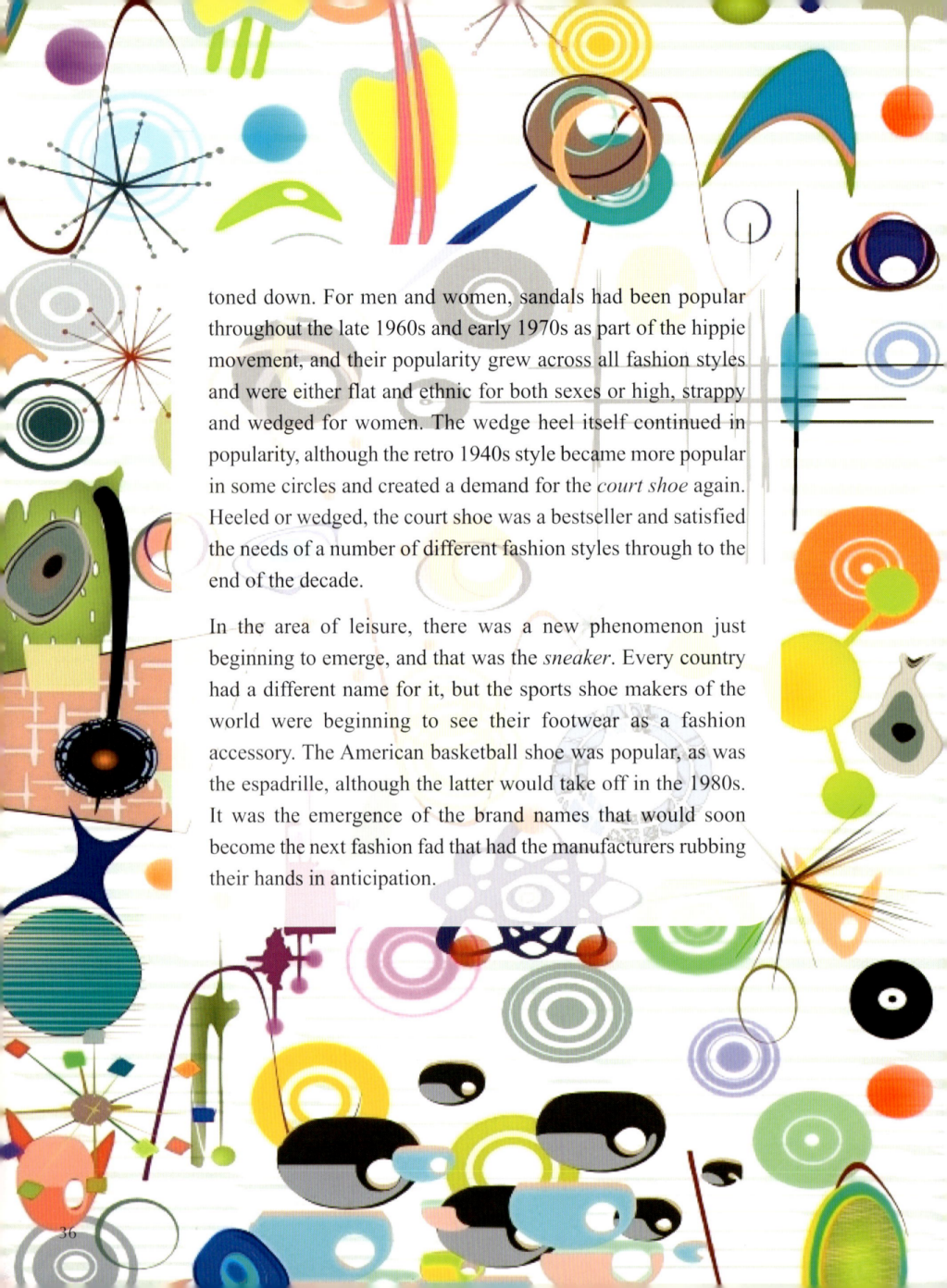

toned down. For men and women, sandals had been popular throughout the late 1960s and early 1970s as part of the hippie movement, and their popularity grew across all fashion styles and were either flat and ethnic for both sexes or high, strappy and wedged for women. The wedge heel itself continued in popularity, although the retro 1940s style became more popular in some circles and created a demand for the *court shoe* again. Heeled or wedged, the court shoe was a bestseller and satisfied the needs of a number of different fashion styles through to the end of the decade.

In the area of leisure, there was a new phenomenon just beginning to emerge, and that was the *sneaker*. Every country had a different name for it, but the sports shoe makers of the world were beginning to see their footwear as a fashion accessory. The American basketball shoe was popular, as was the espadrille, although the latter would take off in the 1980s. It was the emergence of the brand names that would soon become the next fashion fad that had the manufacturers rubbing their hands in anticipation.

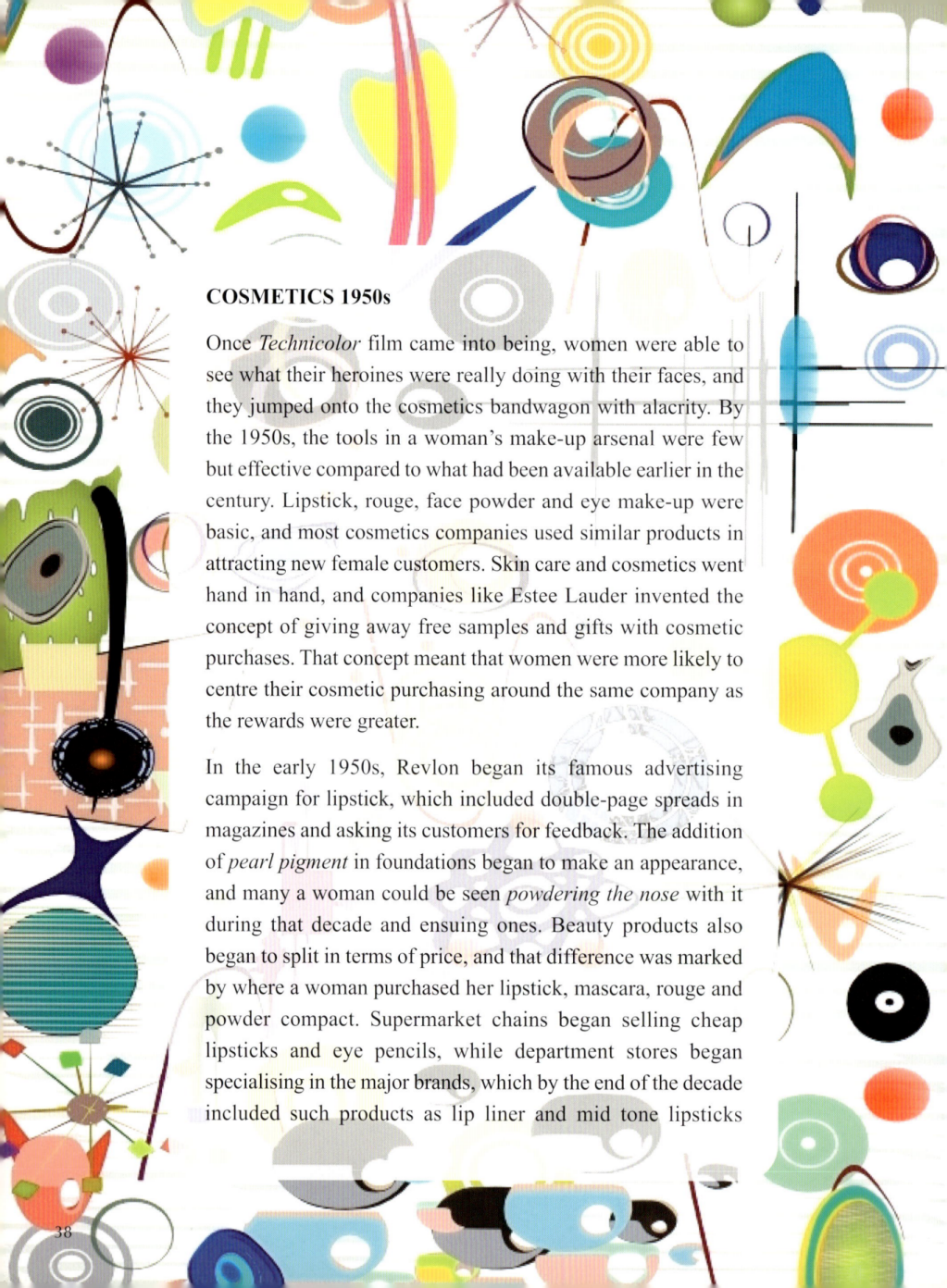

COSMETICS 1950s

Once *Technicolor* film came into being, women were able to see what their heroines were really doing with their faces, and they jumped onto the cosmetics bandwagon with alacrity. By the 1950s, the tools in a woman's make-up arsenal were few but effective compared to what had been available earlier in the century. Lipstick, rouge, face powder and eye make-up were basic, and most cosmetics companies used similar products in attracting new female customers. Skin care and cosmetics went hand in hand, and companies like Estee Lauder invented the concept of giving away free samples and gifts with cosmetic purchases. That concept meant that women were more likely to centre their cosmetic purchasing around the same company as the rewards were greater.

In the early 1950s, Revlon began its famous advertising campaign for lipstick, which included double-page spreads in magazines and asking its customers for feedback. The addition of *pearl pigment* in foundations began to make an appearance, and many a woman could be seen *powdering the nose* with it during that decade and ensuing ones. Beauty products also began to split in terms of price, and that difference was marked by where a woman purchased her lipstick, mascara, rouge and powder compact. Supermarket chains began selling cheap lipsticks and eye pencils, while department stores began specialising in the major brands, which by the end of the decade included such products as lip liner and mid tone lipsticks

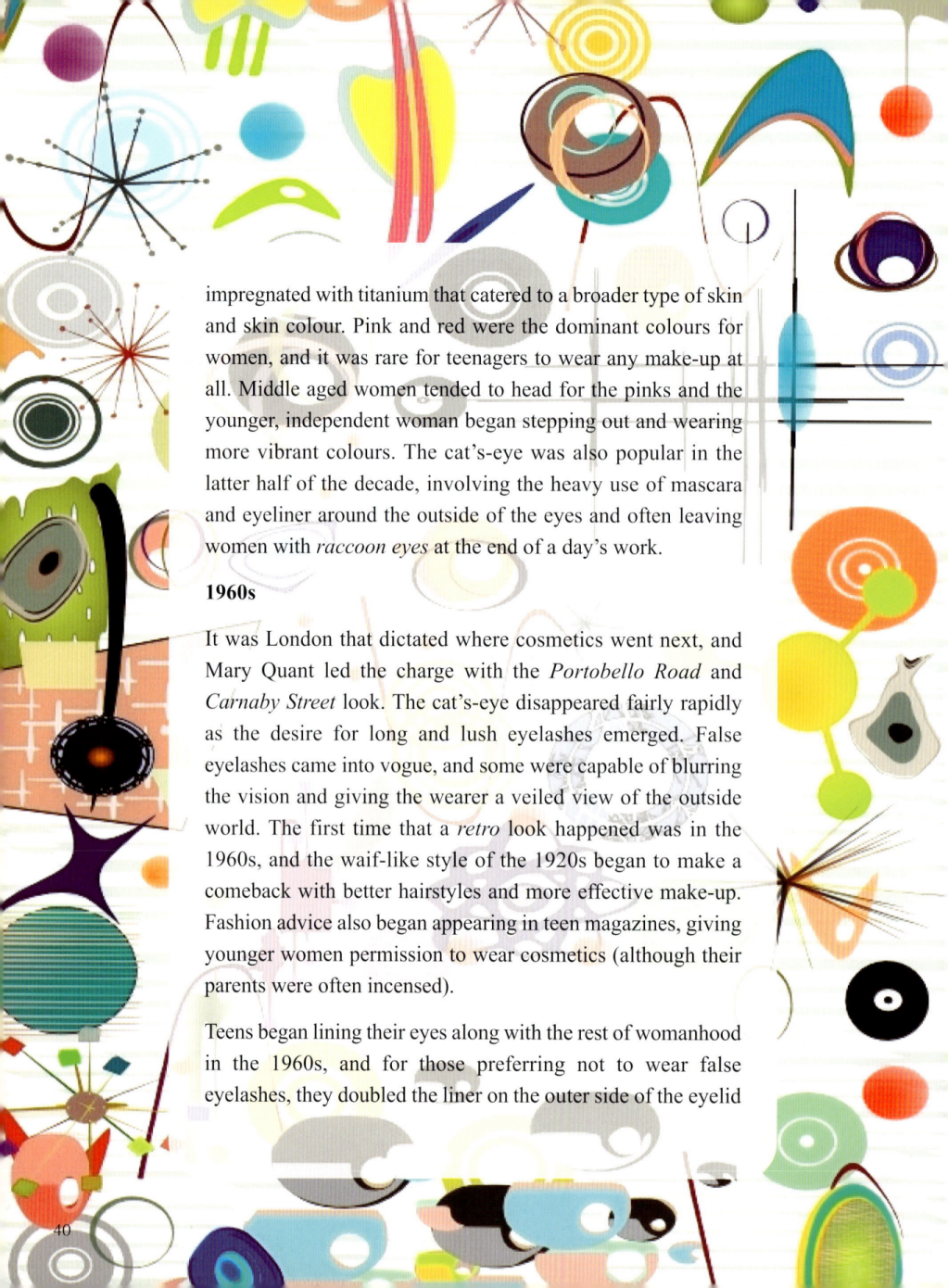

impregnated with titanium that catered to a broader type of skin and skin colour. Pink and red were the dominant colours for women, and it was rare for teenagers to wear any make-up at all. Middle aged women tended to head for the pinks and the younger, independent woman began stepping out and wearing more vibrant colours. The cat's-eye was also popular in the latter half of the decade, involving the heavy use of mascara and eyeliner around the outside of the eyes and often leaving women with *raccoon eyes* at the end of a day's work.

1960s

It was London that dictated where cosmetics went next, and Mary Quant led the charge with the *Portobello Road* and *Carnaby Street* look. The cat's-eye disappeared fairly rapidly as the desire for long and lush eyelashes emerged. False eyelashes came into vogue, and some were capable of blurring the vision and giving the wearer a veiled view of the outside world. The first time that a *retro* look happened was in the 1960s, and the waif-like style of the 1920s began to make a comeback with better hairstyles and more effective make-up. Fashion advice also began appearing in teen magazines, giving younger women permission to wear cosmetics (although their parents were often incensed).

Teens began lining their eyes along with the rest of womanhood in the 1960s, and for those preferring not to wear false eyelashes, they doubled the liner on the outer side of the eyelid

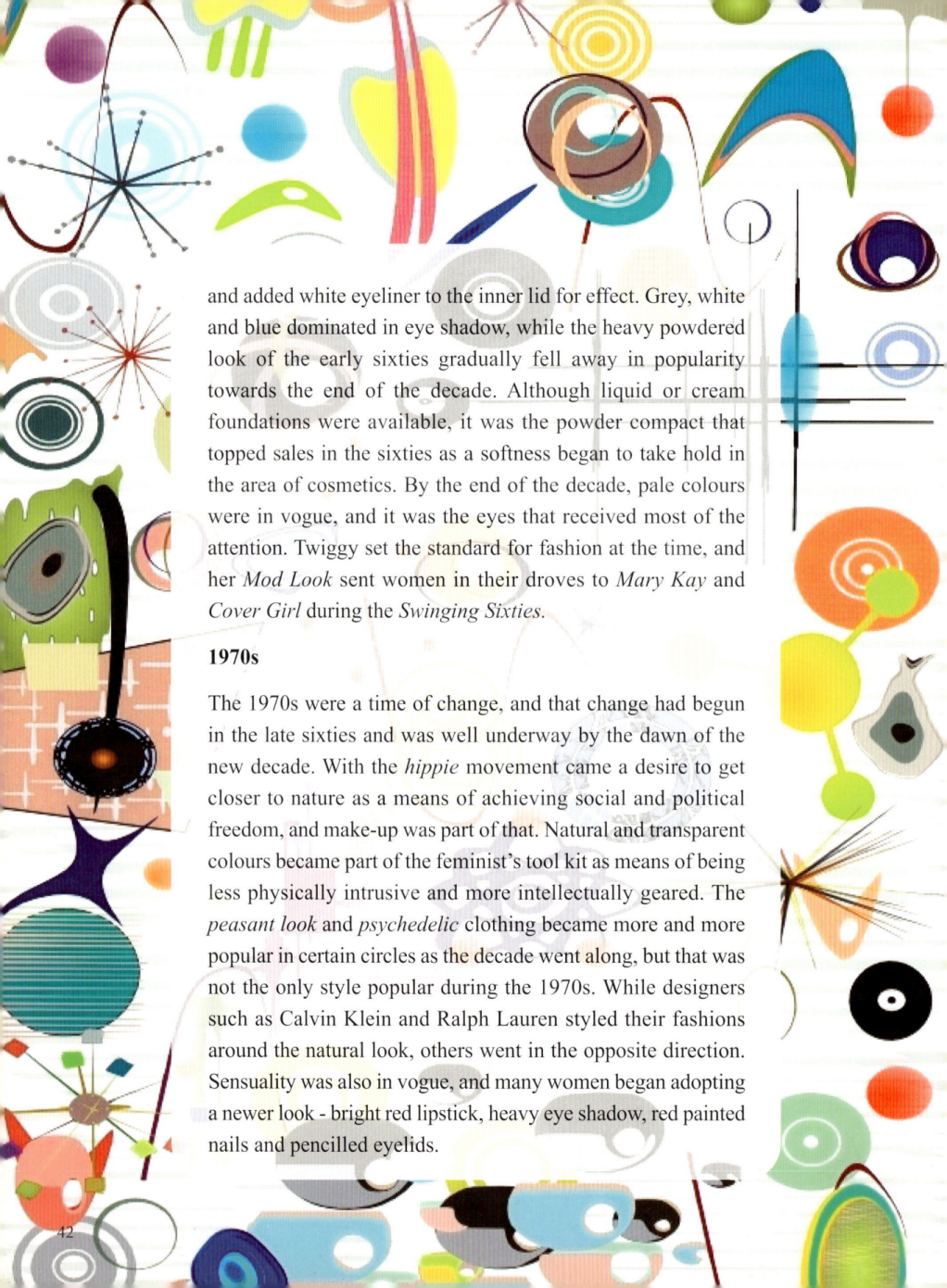

and added white eyeliner to the inner lid for effect. Grey, white and blue dominated in eye shadow, while the heavy powdered look of the early sixties gradually fell away in popularity towards the end of the decade. Although liquid or cream foundations were available, it was the powder compact that topped sales in the sixties as a softness began to take hold in the area of cosmetics. By the end of the decade, pale colours were in vogue, and it was the eyes that received most of the attention. Twiggy set the standard for fashion at the time, and her *Mod Look* sent women in their droves to *Mary Kay* and *Cover Girl* during the *Swinging Sixties*.

1970s

The 1970s were a time of change, and that change had begun in the late sixties and was well underway by the dawn of the new decade. With the *hippie* movement came a desire to get closer to nature as a means of achieving social and political freedom, and make-up was part of that. Natural and transparent colours became part of the feminist's tool kit as means of being less physically intrusive and more intellectually geared. The *peasant look* and *psychedelic* clothing became more and more popular in certain circles as the decade went along, but that was not the only style popular during the 1970s. While designers such as Calvin Klein and Ralph Lauren styled their fashions around the natural look, others went in the opposite direction. Sensuality was also in vogue, and many women began adopting a newer look - bright red lipstick, heavy eye shadow, red painted nails and pencilled eyelids.

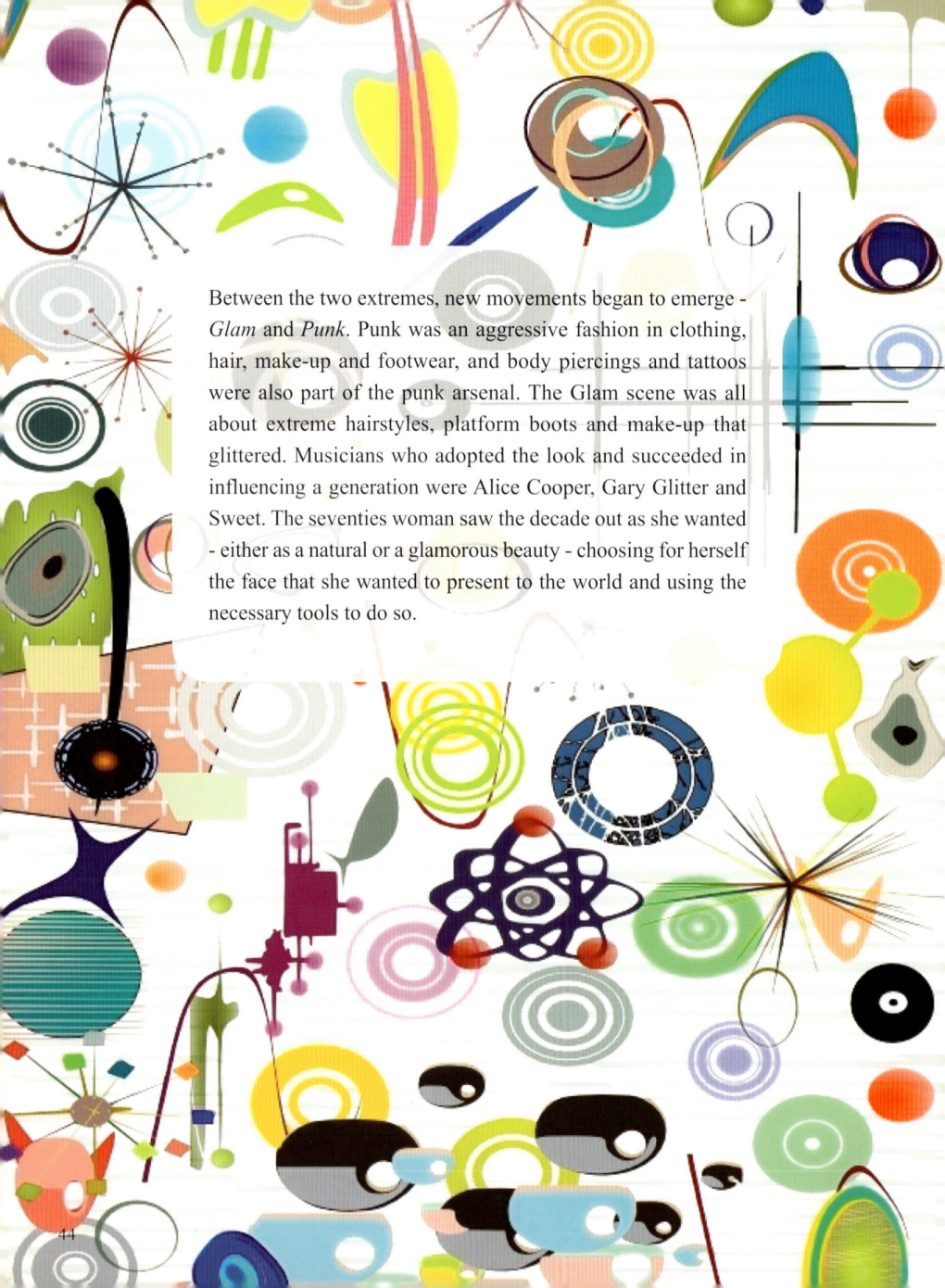

Between the two extremes, new movements began to emerge - *Glam* and *Punk*. Punk was an aggressive fashion in clothing, hair, make-up and footwear, and body piercings and tattoos were also part of the punk arsenal. The Glam scene was all about extreme hairstyles, platform boots and make-up that glittered. Musicians who adopted the look and succeeded in influencing a generation were Alice Cooper, Gary Glitter and Sweet. The seventies woman saw the decade out as she wanted - either as a natural or a glamorous beauty - choosing for herself the face that she wanted to present to the world and using the necessary tools to do so.

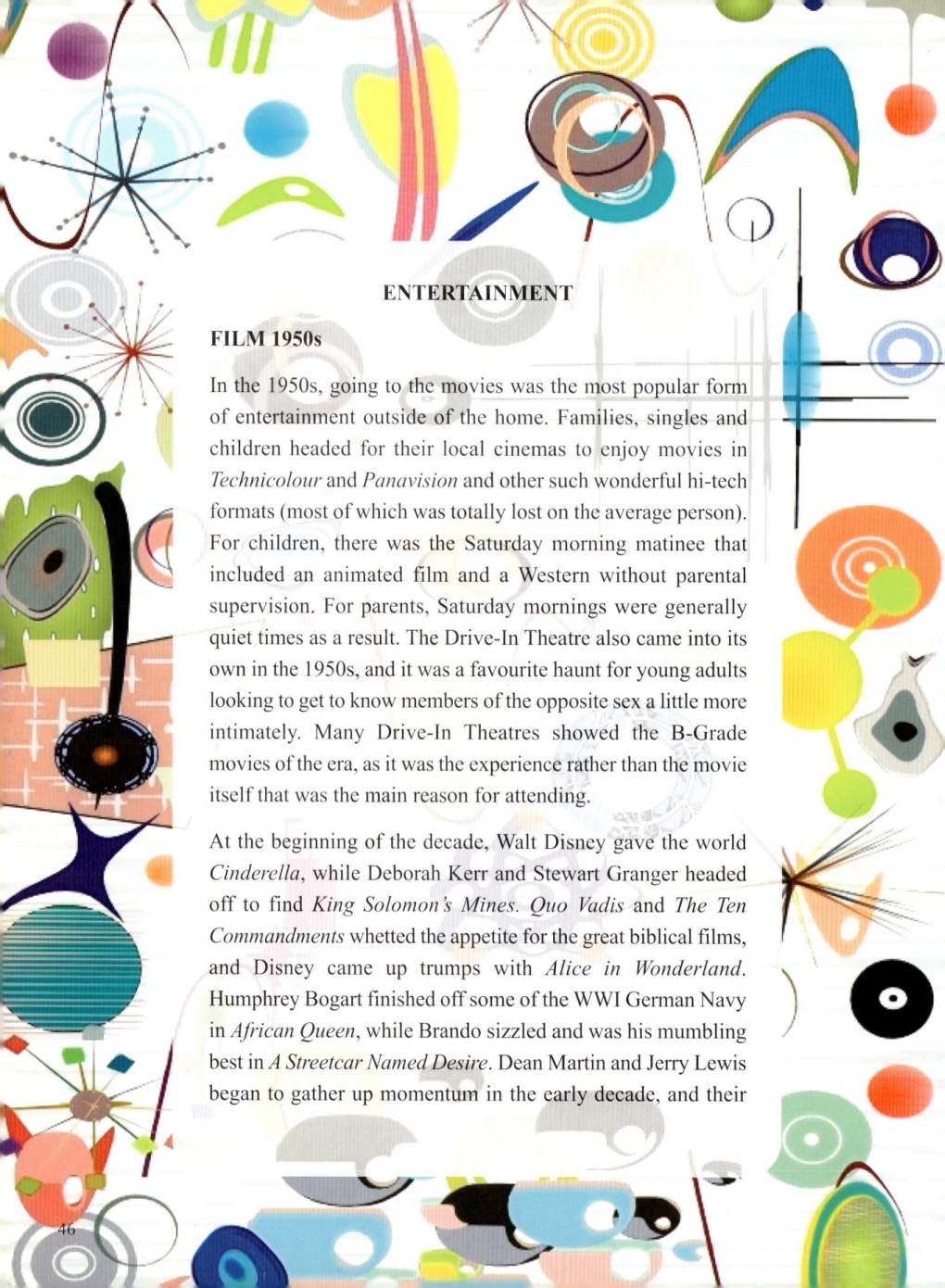

ENTERTAINMENT

FILM 1950s

In the 1950s, going to the movies was the most popular form of entertainment outside of the home. Families, singles and children headed for their local cinemas to enjoy movies in *Technicolour* and *Panavision* and other such wonderful hi-tech formats (most of which was totally lost on the average person). For children, there was the Saturday morning matinee that included an animated film and a Western without parental supervision. For parents, Saturday mornings were generally quiet times as a result. The Drive-In Theatre also came into its own in the 1950s, and it was a favourite haunt for young adults looking to get to know members of the opposite sex a little more intimately. Many Drive-In Theatres showed the B-Grade movies of the era, as it was the experience rather than the movie itself that was the main reason for attending.

At the beginning of the decade, Walt Disney gave the world *Cinderella*, while Deborah Kerr and Stewart Granger headed off to find *King Solomon's Mines*. *Quo Vadis* and *The Ten Commandments* whetted the appetite for the great biblical films, and Disney came up trumps with *Alice in Wonderland*. Humphrey Bogart finished off some of the WWI German Navy in *African Queen*, while Brando sizzled and was his mumbling best in *A Streetcar Named Desire*. Dean Martin and Jerry Lewis began to gather up momentum in the early decade, and their

brand of comedy often a welcome change after watching such epics as *From Here to Eternity*, *Shane* and *On the Waterfront*. Musicals were also very popular, as was Marilyn Monroe. *Gentlemen Prefer Blondes*, *The Seven Year Itch* and *Some Like it Hot* were Monroe's highest grossing movies in the 1950s. Alfred Hitchcock kept a generation of movie-goers on the edges of their seats with *Rear Window* and *Dial M for Murder*; Elvis gyrated his way through *Jailhouse Rock* and a number of other same-script-different-set movies that the fans loved, and James Dean left far too soon. The fifties left the world spoiled for choice in movies, and as the industry was still in its formative years, it augured well for the future. Animation, musicals, serious religious productions and light-hearted entertainment was available to the masses, and they couldn't get enough of it. Stars such as Bing Crosby, David Niven, Gordon MacRae, Shirley Jones and Audrey Hepburn gave us laughter and lifted the spirits of all but the very cynical. Kirk Douglas, Peter Lorre, James Mason, Alec Guinness, Burt Lancaster and William Holden had us waiting until the very last moment until good triumphed over bad and all was revealed.

The movies were the great escape for the public in the 1950s, and for many, it was an experience never to be forgotten. For children, it was a time to dream and to head out of the cinema with all guns blazing. For lovers, it was a hidden world where stolen endearments in the dark were precious moments that ended all too soon.

1960s

By the time the 1960s dawned, Hollywood and Britain were old hands at knowing what the general public wanted to see on celluloid, and they turned out virtually every type of movie imaginable. Never again would a 20th century decade see people enjoy such a wide range of high quality productions and actors, and the list of award winning movies includes the who's who of the best performers ever to grace the screen. One of the greatest thrillers ever made came in the form of *Psycho*, followed closely by Hitchcock's *The Birds*. The Horror Movie also took a step up the ladder of terrifying believability with *Rosemary's Baby* for those who could stomach it. The 1960s was also a time for family movies, as well as many other genres, and some of the greats of the decade were *The Sound of Music*, *Those Magnificent Men in Their Flying Machines*, *My Fair Lady* and *Mary Poppins*.

Laughter came by the bucketful as well, and from both sides of the Atlantic. Peter Sellers brought his unique and side splitting humour to life with *The Pink Panther* and *A Shot in the Dark*, while the Rat Pack delivered one more classic in the form of *Ocean's 11*. The sixties was the time of Doris Day, who never failed to entertain, as did Jack Lemon and Walter Matthau when they arrived as *The Odd Couple*. Another great contributor that continues to thrill today is *Bond*, and Sean Connery first gave us the man with the License to Kill in *Dr. No* and continued on through the decade. *The Jungle Book* entertained then as it

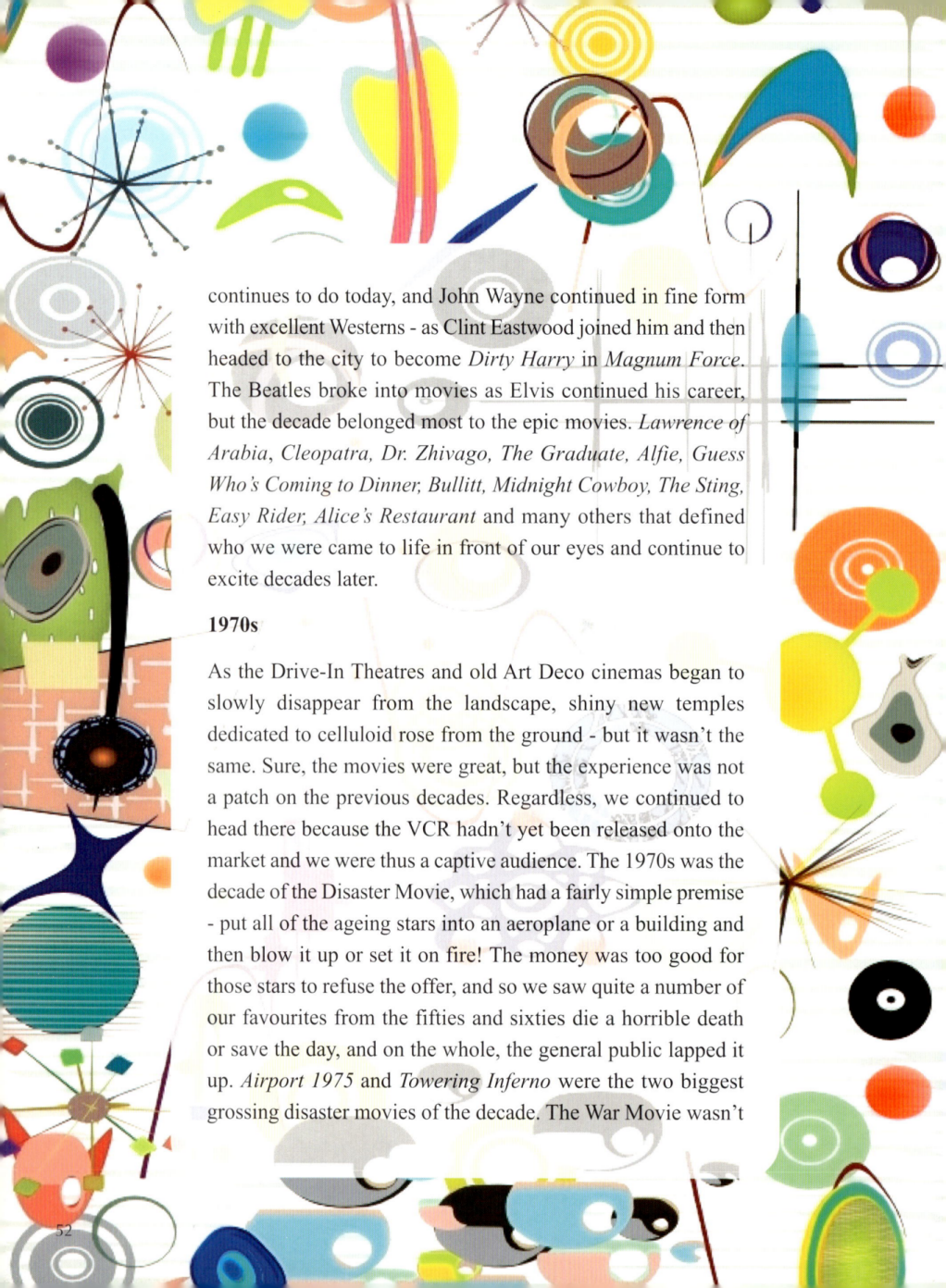

continues to do today, and John Wayne continued in fine form with excellent Westerns - as Clint Eastwood joined him and then headed to the city to become *Dirty Harry* in *Magnum Force*. The Beatles broke into movies as Elvis continued his career, but the decade belonged most to the epic movies. *Lawrence of Arabia*, *Cleopatra*, *Dr. Zhivago*, *The Graduate*, *Alfie*, *Guess Who's Coming to Dinner*, *Bullitt*, *Midnight Cowboy*, *The Sting*, *Easy Rider*, *Alice's Restaurant* and many others that defined who we were came to life in front of our eyes and continue to excite decades later.

1970s

As the Drive-In Theatres and old Art Deco cinemas began to slowly disappear from the landscape, shiny new temples dedicated to celluloid rose from the ground - but it wasn't the same. Sure, the movies were great, but the experience was not a patch on the previous decades. Regardless, we continued to head there because the VCR hadn't yet been released onto the market and we were thus a captive audience. The 1970s was the decade of the Disaster Movie, which had a fairly simple premise - put all of the ageing stars into an aeroplane or a building and then blow it up or set it on fire! The money was too good for those stars to refuse the offer, and so we saw quite a number of our favourites from the fifties and sixties die a horrible death or save the day, and on the whole, the general public lapped it up. *Airport 1975* and *Towering Inferno* were the two biggest grossing disaster movies of the decade. The War Movie wasn't

as popular as it had once been, but a lot of that was down to the ongoing Vietnam War and its unpopularity. Nevertheless, the stars came out to give us *Tora! Tora! Tora!* and *Midway*, as well as *M*A*S*H*, which blended humour with a serious subject and inspired one of the most successful TV series ever.

Bond continued to thrill through the decade, and Roger Moore brought the house down in the opening scene of *The Spy Who Loved Me*. The 1970s also brought us the wonderful humour of Mel Brooks and the *Smokey and the Bandit* movies. It was *Jaws* however that broke box office records, along with the terrifying offerings of *The Exorcist* and *The Amityville Horror* and Stallone in the first of the *Rocky* movies. Thankfully, John Travolta was on hand to give us some *Saturday Night Fever*, and for those who were into Sci Fi, there was *Star Wars, Alien* and *Close Encounters of the Third Kind*. It would be some time before quality cinema was available in such quantities as the 1970s gave us, and as the VCR arrived, we were able to hire and re-watch such 1970s classics as *Kramer vs. Kramer, The Godfather, The Sting, American Graffiti, Love Story* and *One Flew Over the Cuckoo's Nest*.

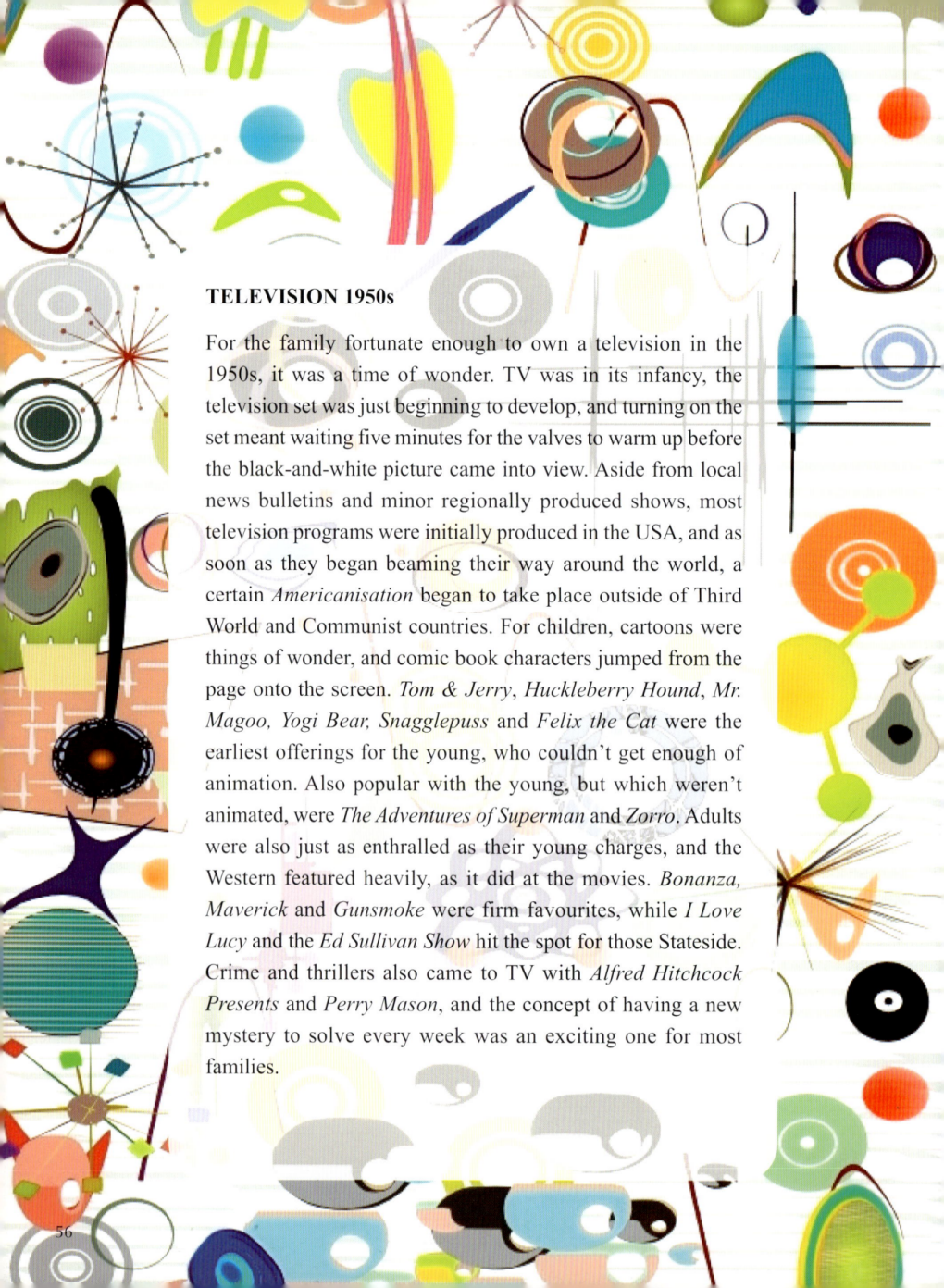

TELEVISION 1950s

For the family fortunate enough to own a television in the 1950s, it was a time of wonder. TV was in its infancy, the television set was just beginning to develop, and turning on the set meant waiting five minutes for the valves to warm up before the black-and-white picture came into view. Aside from local news bulletins and minor regionally produced shows, most television programs were initially produced in the USA, and as soon as they began beaming their way around the world, a certain *Americanisation* began to take place outside of Third World and Communist countries. For children, cartoons were things of wonder, and comic book characters jumped from the page onto the screen. *Tom & Jerry*, *Huckleberry Hound*, *Mr. Magoo*, *Yogi Bear*, *Snagglepuss* and *Felix the Cat* were the earliest offerings for the young, who couldn't get enough of animation. Also popular with the young, but which weren't animated, were *The Adventures of Superman* and *Zorro*. Adults were also just as enthralled as their young charges, and the Western featured heavily, as it did at the movies. *Bonanza*, *Maverick* and *Gunsmoke* were firm favourites, while *I Love Lucy* and the *Ed Sullivan Show* hit the spot for those Stateside. Crime and thrillers also came to TV with *Alfred Hitchcock Presents* and *Perry Mason*, and the concept of having a new mystery to solve every week was an exciting one for most families.

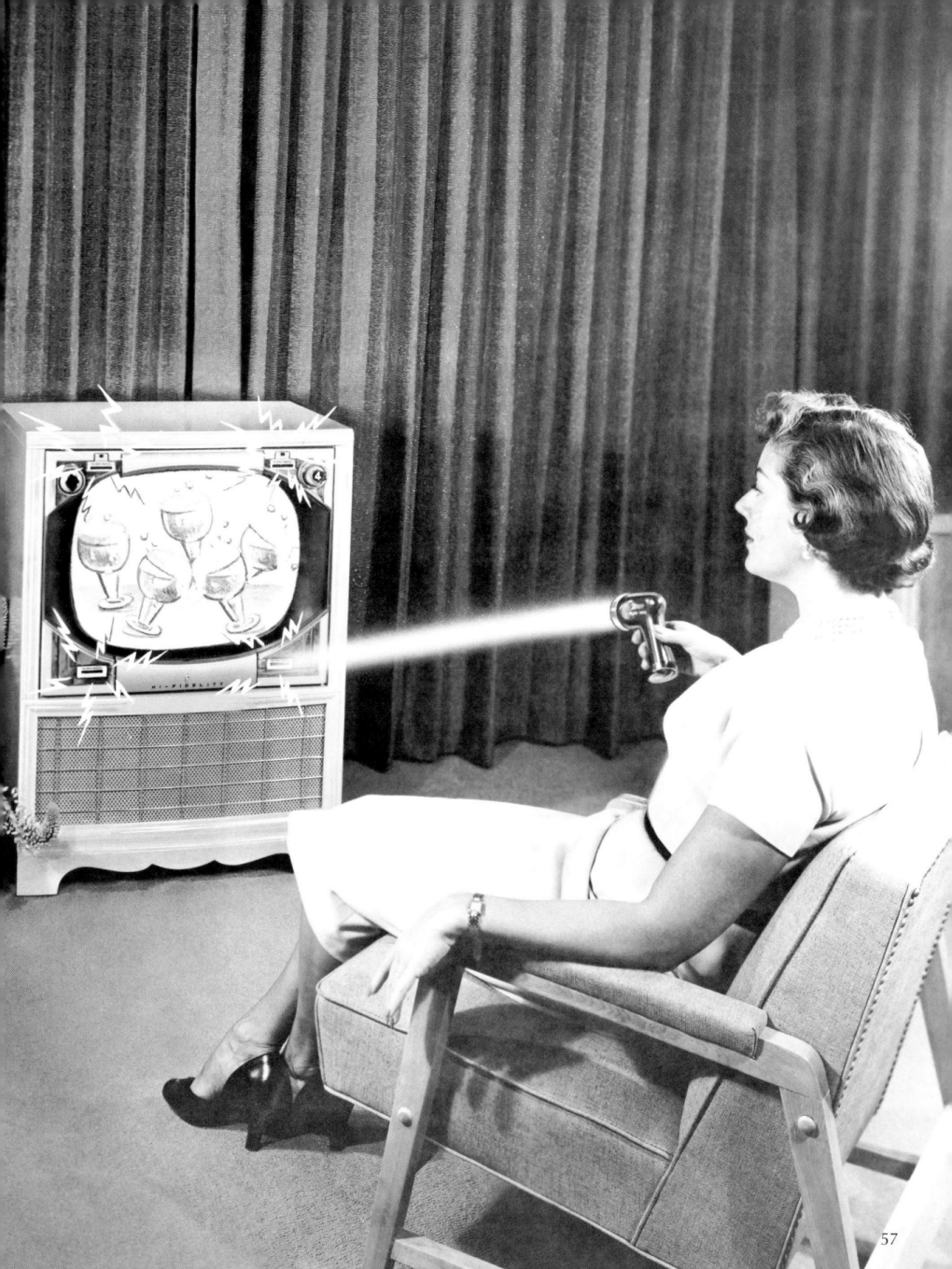

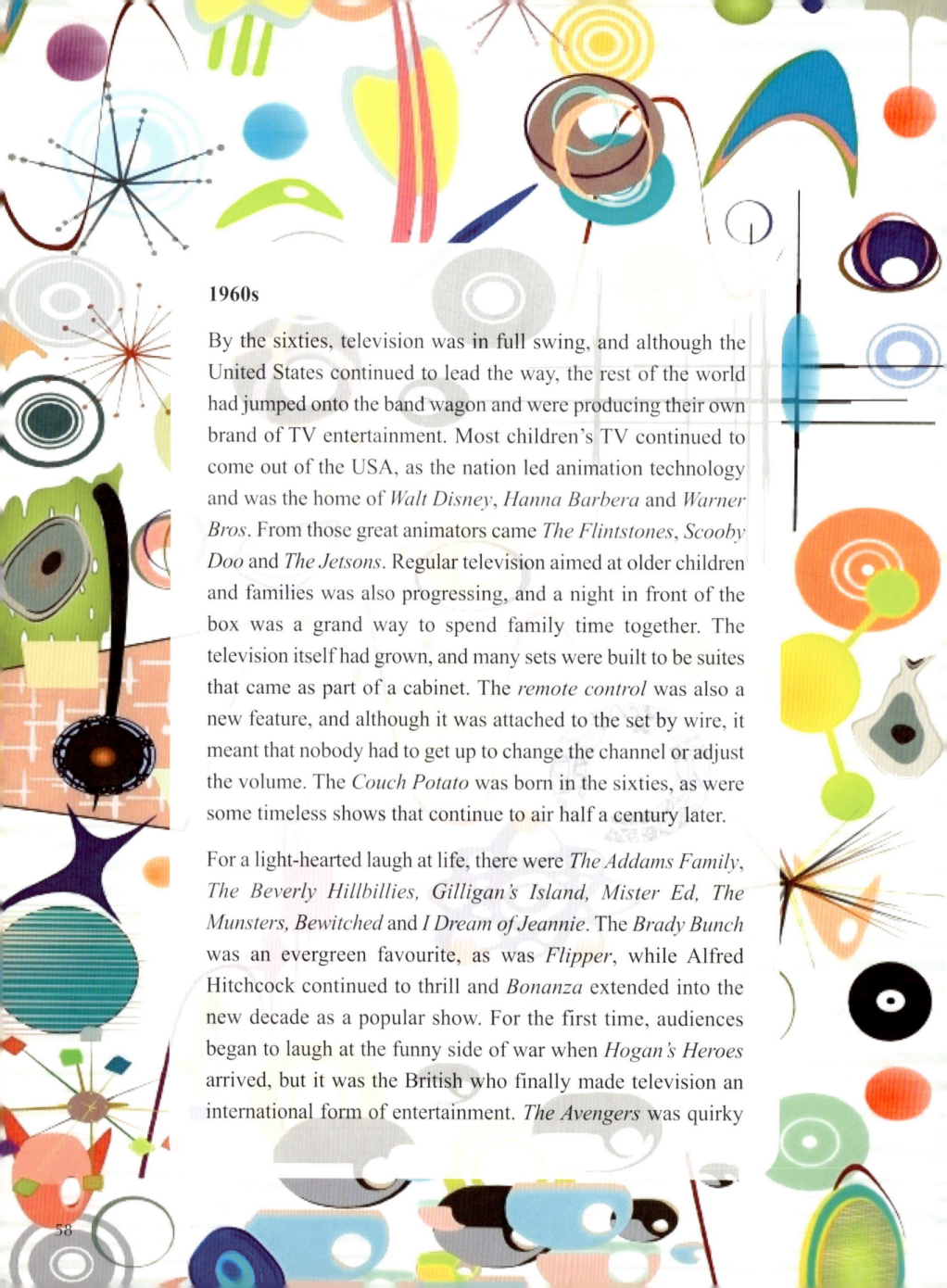

1960s

By the sixties, television was in full swing, and although the United States continued to lead the way, the rest of the world had jumped onto the band wagon and were producing their own brand of TV entertainment. Most children's TV continued to come out of the USA, as the nation led animation technology and was the home of *Walt Disney*, *Hanna Barbera* and *Warner Bros*. From those great animators came *The Flintstones*, *Scooby Doo* and *The Jetsons*. Regular television aimed at older children and families was also progressing, and a night in front of the box was a grand way to spend family time together. The television itself had grown, and many sets were built to be suites that came as part of a cabinet. The *remote control* was also a new feature, and although it was attached to the set by wire, it meant that nobody had to get up to change the channel or adjust the volume. The *Couch Potato* was born in the sixties, as were some timeless shows that continue to air half a century later.

For a light-hearted laugh at life, there were *The Addams Family*, *The Beverly Hillbillies*, *Gilligan's Island*, *Mister Ed*, *The Munsters*, *Bewitched* and *I Dream of Jeannie*. The *Brady Bunch* was an evergreen favourite, as was *Flipper*, while Alfred Hitchcock continued to thrill and *Bonanza* extended into the new decade as a popular show. For the first time, audiences began to laugh at the funny side of war when *Hogan's Heroes* arrived, but it was the British who finally made television an international form of entertainment. *The Avengers* was quirky

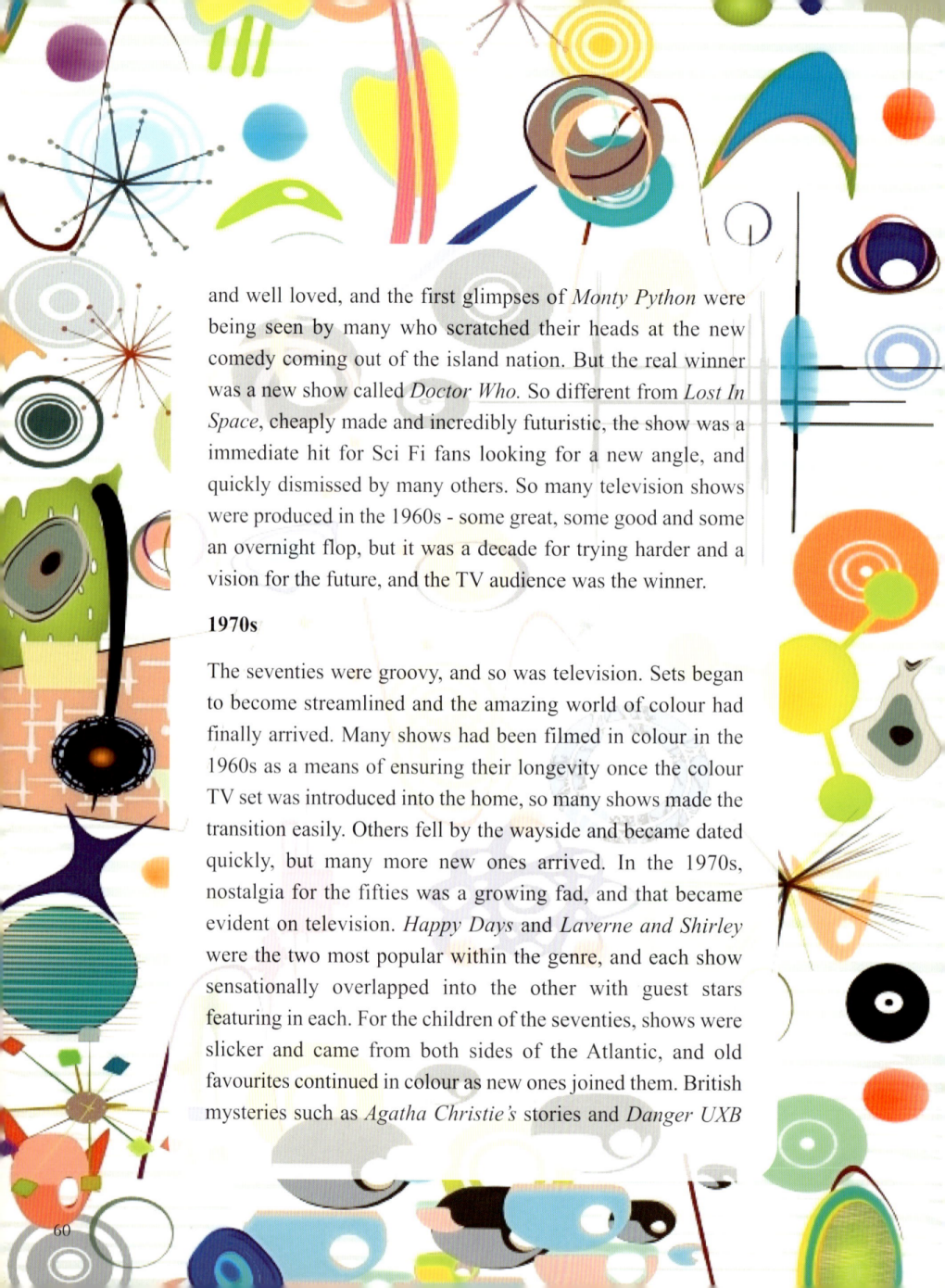

and well loved, and the first glimpses of *Monty Python* were being seen by many who scratched their heads at the new comedy coming out of the island nation. But the real winner was a new show called *Doctor Who.* So different from *Lost In Space*, cheaply made and incredibly futuristic, the show was a immediate hit for Sci Fi fans looking for a new angle, and quickly dismissed by many others. So many television shows were produced in the 1960s - some great, some good and some an overnight flop, but it was a decade for trying harder and a vision for the future, and the TV audience was the winner.

1970s

The seventies were groovy, and so was television. Sets began to become streamlined and the amazing world of colour had finally arrived. Many shows had been filmed in colour in the 1960s as a means of ensuring their longevity once the colour TV set was introduced into the home, so many shows made the transition easily. Others fell by the wayside and became dated quickly, but many more new ones arrived. In the 1970s, nostalgia for the fifties was a growing fad, and that became evident on television. *Happy Days* and *Laverne and Shirley* were the two most popular within the genre, and each show sensationally overlapped into the other with guest stars featuring in each. For the children of the seventies, shows were slicker and came from both sides of the Atlantic, and old favourites continued in colour as new ones joined them. British mysteries such as *Agatha Christie's* stories and *Danger UXB*

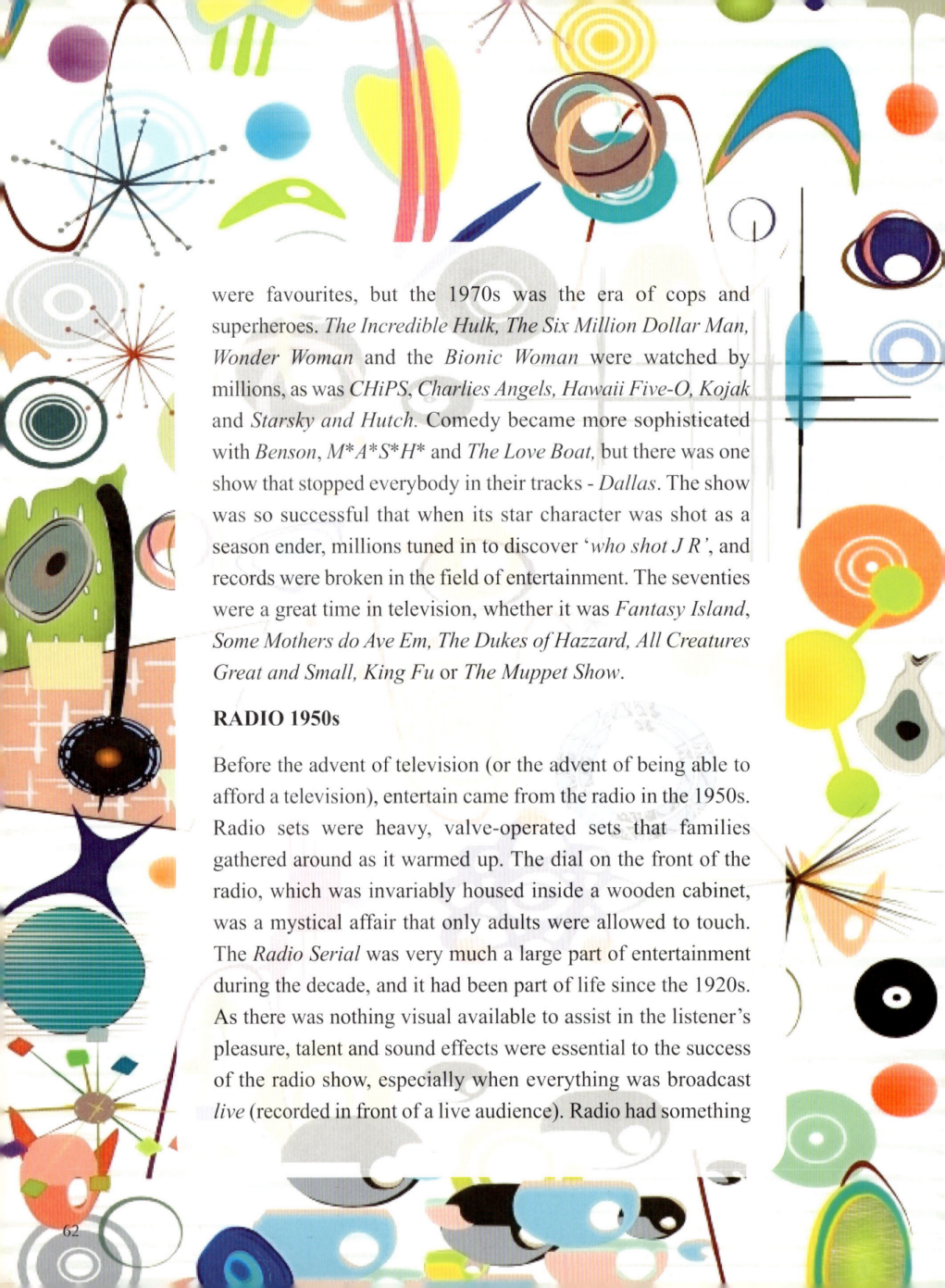

were favourites, but the 1970s was the era of cops and superheroes. *The Incredible Hulk, The Six Million Dollar Man, Wonder Woman* and the *Bionic Woman* were watched by millions, as was *CHiPS, Charlies Angels, Hawaii Five-O, Kojak* and *Starsky and Hutch.* Comedy became more sophisticated with *Benson, M*A*S*H** and *The Love Boat,* but there was one show that stopped everybody in their tracks - *Dallas.* The show was so successful that when its star character was shot as a season ender, millions tuned in to discover '*who shot J R'*, and records were broken in the field of entertainment. The seventies were a great time in television, whether it was *Fantasy Island, Some Mothers do Ave Em, The Dukes of Hazzard, All Creatures Great and Small, King Fu* or *The Muppet Show.*

RADIO 1950s

Before the advent of television (or the advent of being able to afford a television), entertain came from the radio in the 1950s. Radio sets were heavy, valve-operated sets that families gathered around as it warmed up. The dial on the front of the radio, which was invariably housed inside a wooden cabinet, was a mystical affair that only adults were allowed to touch. The *Radio Serial* was very much a large part of entertainment during the decade, and it had been part of life since the 1920s. As there was nothing visual available to assist in the listener's pleasure, talent and sound effects were essential to the success of the radio show, especially when everything was broadcast *live* (recorded in front of a live audience). Radio had something

to offer the family for the entire day and most of the evening, and after a certain time, morning radio was aimed at the home maker who listened as she went about her chores. Music to work to and early soapies took up most of the morning, and lunchtime generally arrived with a light drama of one sort or another. Advertising subliminally dictated the family's shopping list throughout the afternoon as music saw things through to the arrival of children and the husband for the nightly ritual of feeding and bathing before the whole family sat down to listen together.

In the evenings, families warmed up the set again and settled in for chat shows, boxing matches, big bands and variety theatre. Comedy was a huge favourite, as were competitions and listeners' requests (which were entered through the mail). Some of television's stars began their careers on the radio. Censorship was fairly strict at the time, although there was very little available for children in the early days. That soon changed when the serial Westerns came on, and by the end of the decade, children were laughing just as hard as their parents to some of their favourite shows. Another great revolution began in the second half of the decade with the birth of Rock-and-Roll, and new stations began popping up, dedicated specifically to the lucrative teen market and with advertising targeting a brand new consumer demographic. From the moment the strains of *Rock Around the Clock* were first heard on radio, the medium and the entire industry changed forever, and the young began to dictate where radio went next.

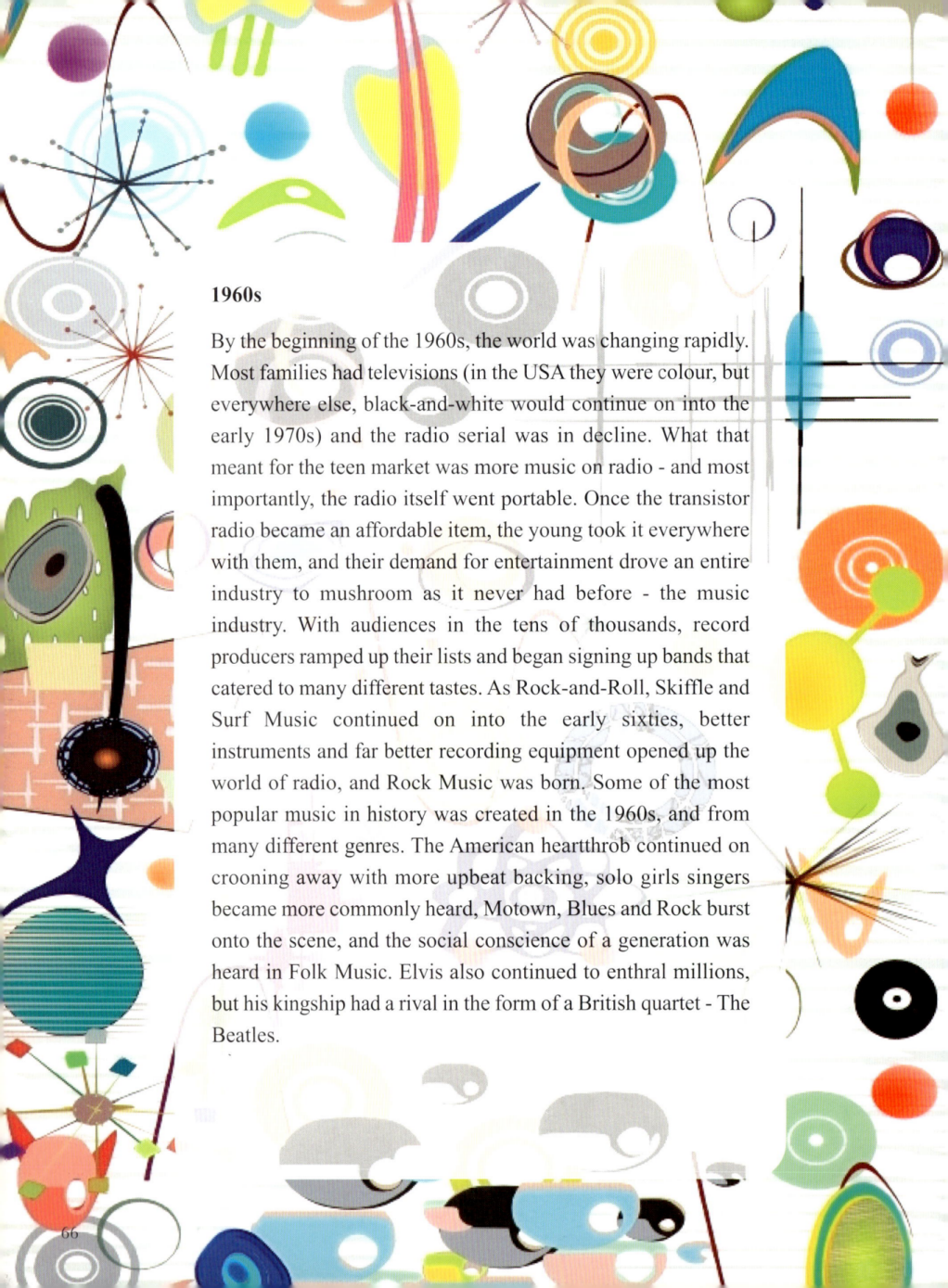

1960s

By the beginning of the 1960s, the world was changing rapidly. Most families had televisions (in the USA they were colour, but everywhere else, black-and-white would continue on into the early 1970s) and the radio serial was in decline. What that meant for the teen market was more music on radio - and most importantly, the radio itself went portable. Once the transistor radio became an affordable item, the young took it everywhere with them, and their demand for entertainment drove an entire industry to mushroom as it never had before - the music industry. With audiences in the tens of thousands, record producers ramped up their lists and began signing up bands that catered to many different tastes. As Rock-and-Roll, Skiffle and Surf Music continued on into the early sixties, better instruments and far better recording equipment opened up the world of radio, and Rock Music was born. Some of the most popular music in history was created in the 1960s, and from many different genres. The American heartthrob continued on crooning away with more upbeat backing, solo girls singers became more commonly heard, Motown, Blues and Rock burst onto the scene, and the social conscience of a generation was heard in Folk Music. Elvis also continued to enthral millions, but his kingship had a rival in the form of a British quartet - The Beatles.

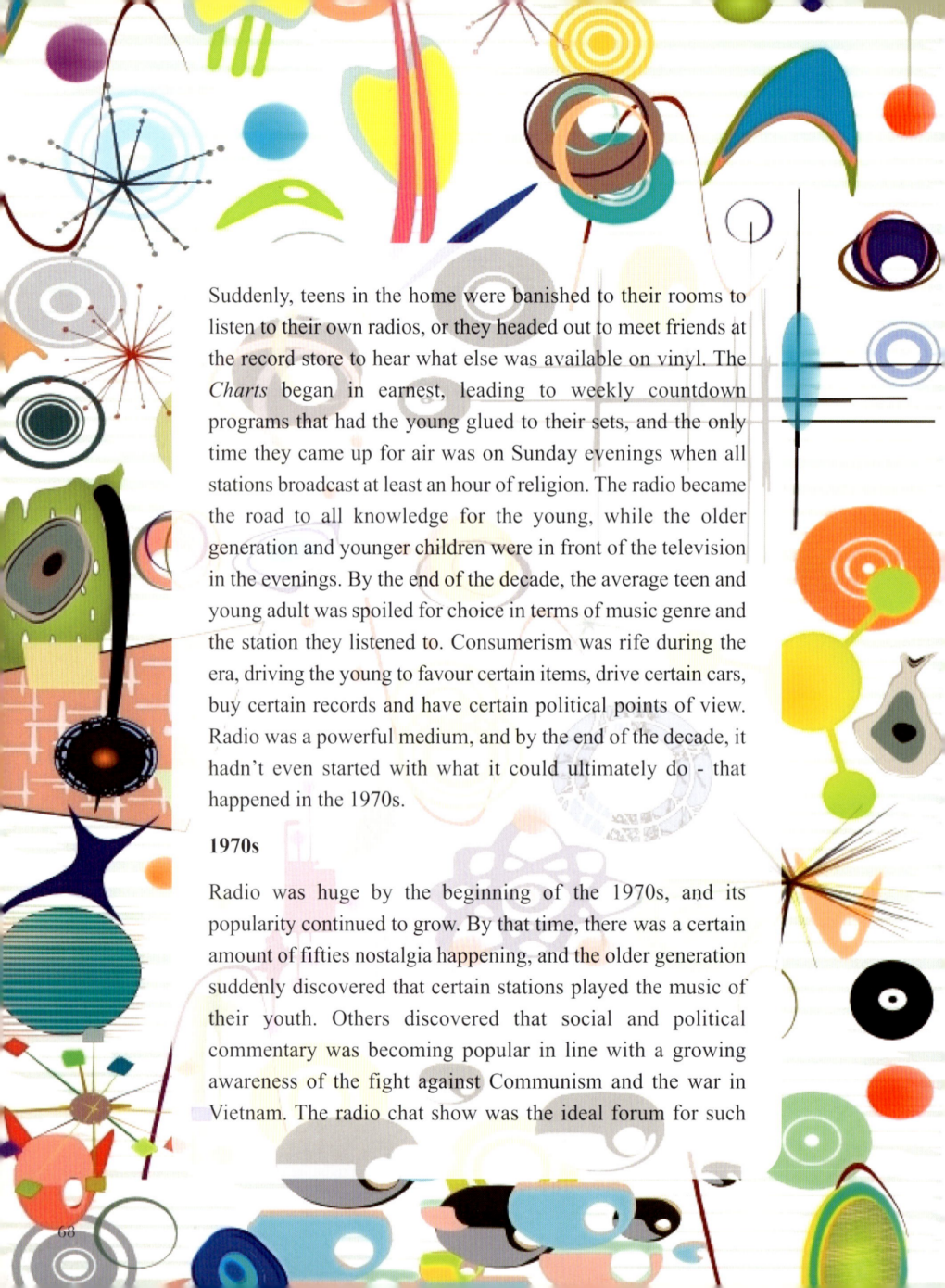

Suddenly, teens in the home were banished to their rooms to listen to their own radios, or they headed out to meet friends at the record store to hear what else was available on vinyl. The *Charts* began in earnest, leading to weekly countdown programs that had the young glued to their sets, and the only time they came up for air was on Sunday evenings when all stations broadcast at least an hour of religion. The radio became the road to all knowledge for the young, while the older generation and younger children were in front of the television in the evenings. By the end of the decade, the average teen and young adult was spoiled for choice in terms of music genre and the station they listened to. Consumerism was rife during the era, driving the young to favour certain items, drive certain cars, buy certain records and have certain political points of view. Radio was a powerful medium, and by the end of the decade, it hadn't even started with what it could ultimately do - that happened in the 1970s.

1970s

Radio was huge by the beginning of the 1970s, and its popularity continued to grow. By that time, there was a certain amount of fifties nostalgia happening, and the older generation suddenly discovered that certain stations played the music of their youth. Others discovered that social and political commentary was becoming popular in line with a growing awareness of the fight against Communism and the war in Vietnam. The radio chat show was the ideal forum for such

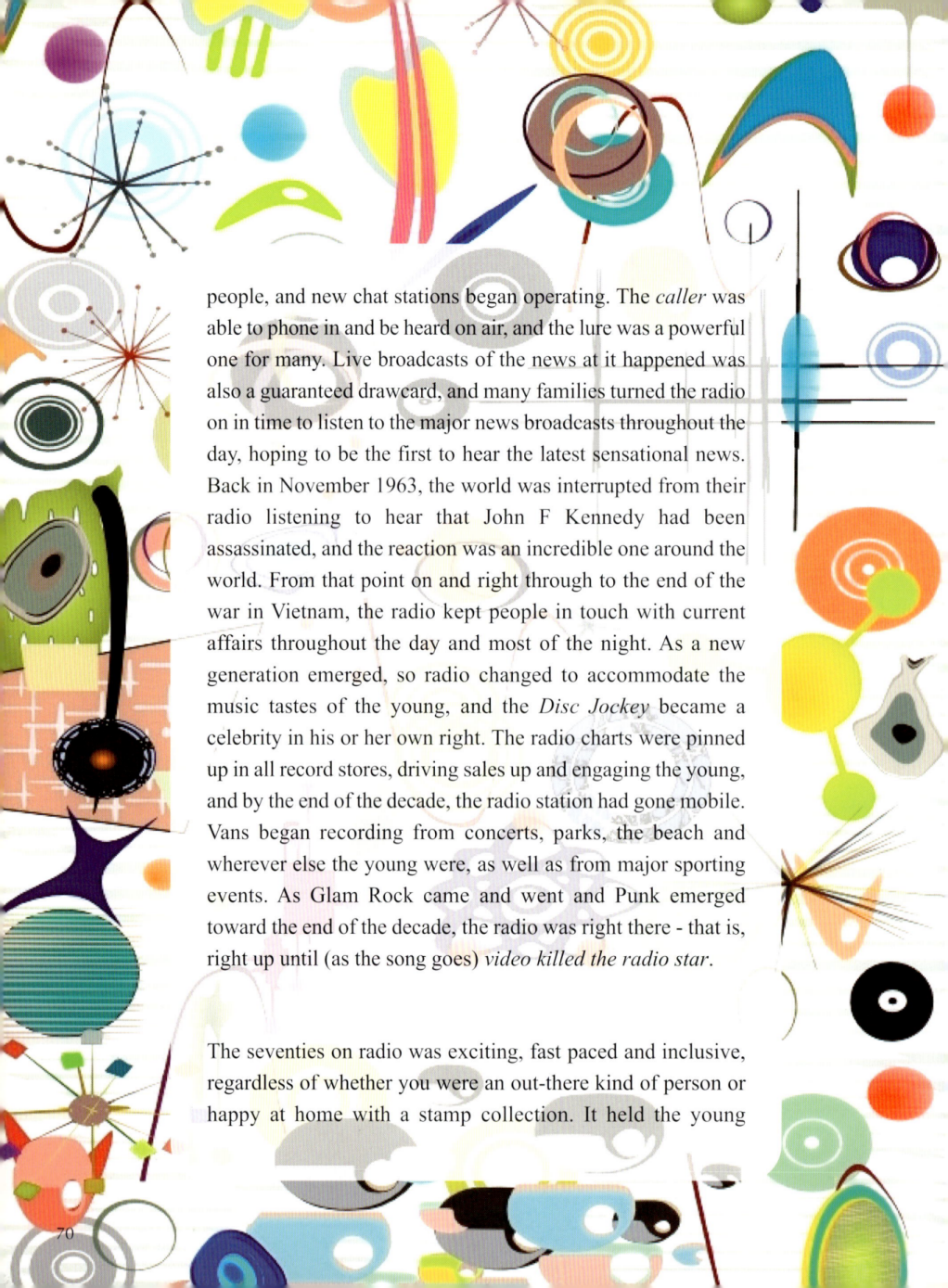

people, and new chat stations began operating. The *caller* was able to phone in and be heard on air, and the lure was a powerful one for many. Live broadcasts of the news at it happened was also a guaranteed drawcard, and many families turned the radio on in time to listen to the major news broadcasts throughout the day, hoping to be the first to hear the latest sensational news. Back in November 1963, the world was interrupted from their radio listening to hear that John F Kennedy had been assassinated, and the reaction was an incredible one around the world. From that point on and right through to the end of the war in Vietnam, the radio kept people in touch with current affairs throughout the day and most of the night. As a new generation emerged, so radio changed to accommodate the music tastes of the young, and the *Disc Jockey* became a celebrity in his or her own right. The radio charts were pinned up in all record stores, driving sales up and engaging the young, and by the end of the decade, the radio station had gone mobile. Vans began recording from concerts, parks, the beach and wherever else the young were, as well as from major sporting events. As Glam Rock came and went and Punk emerged toward the end of the decade, the radio was right there - that is, right up until (as the song goes) *video killed the radio star*.

The seventies on radio was exciting, fast paced and inclusive, regardless of whether you were an out-there kind of person or happy at home with a stamp collection. It held the young

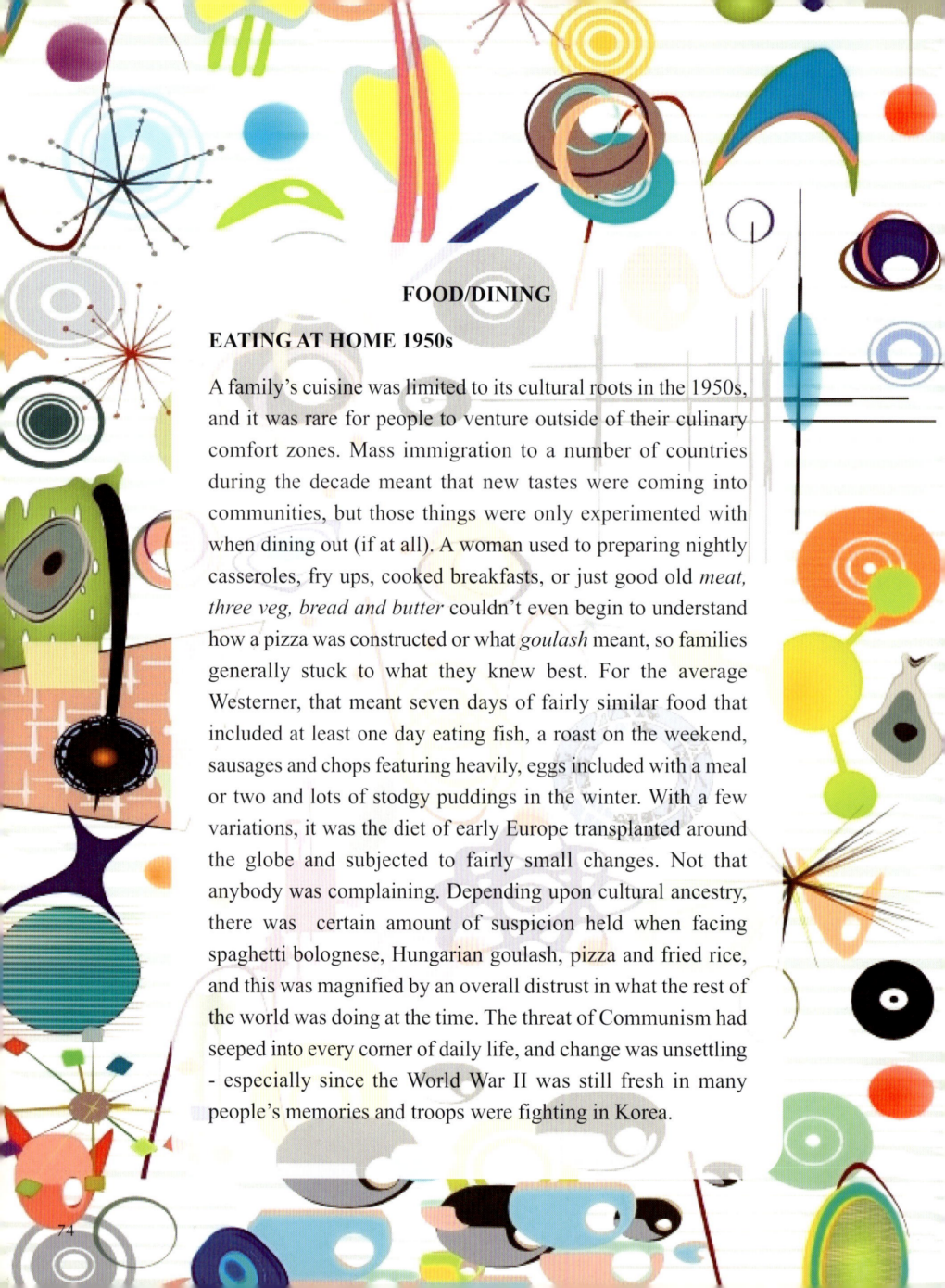

FOOD/DINING

EATING AT HOME 1950s

A family's cuisine was limited to its cultural roots in the 1950s, and it was rare for people to venture outside of their culinary comfort zones. Mass immigration to a number of countries during the decade meant that new tastes were coming into communities, but those things were only experimented with when dining out (if at all). A woman used to preparing nightly casseroles, fry ups, cooked breakfasts, or just good old *meat, three veg, bread and butter* couldn't even begin to understand how a pizza was constructed or what *goulash* meant, so families generally stuck to what they knew best. For the average Westerner, that meant seven days of fairly similar food that included at least one day eating fish, a roast on the weekend, sausages and chops featuring heavily, eggs included with a meal or two and lots of stodgy puddings in the winter. With a few variations, it was the diet of early Europe transplanted around the globe and subjected to fairly small changes. Not that anybody was complaining. Depending upon cultural ancestry, there was a certain amount of suspicion held when facing spaghetti bolognese, Hungarian goulash, pizza and fried rice, and this was magnified by an overall distrust in what the rest of the world was doing at the time. The threat of Communism had seeped into every corner of daily life, and change was unsettling - especially since the World War II was still fresh in many people's memories and troops were fighting in Korea.

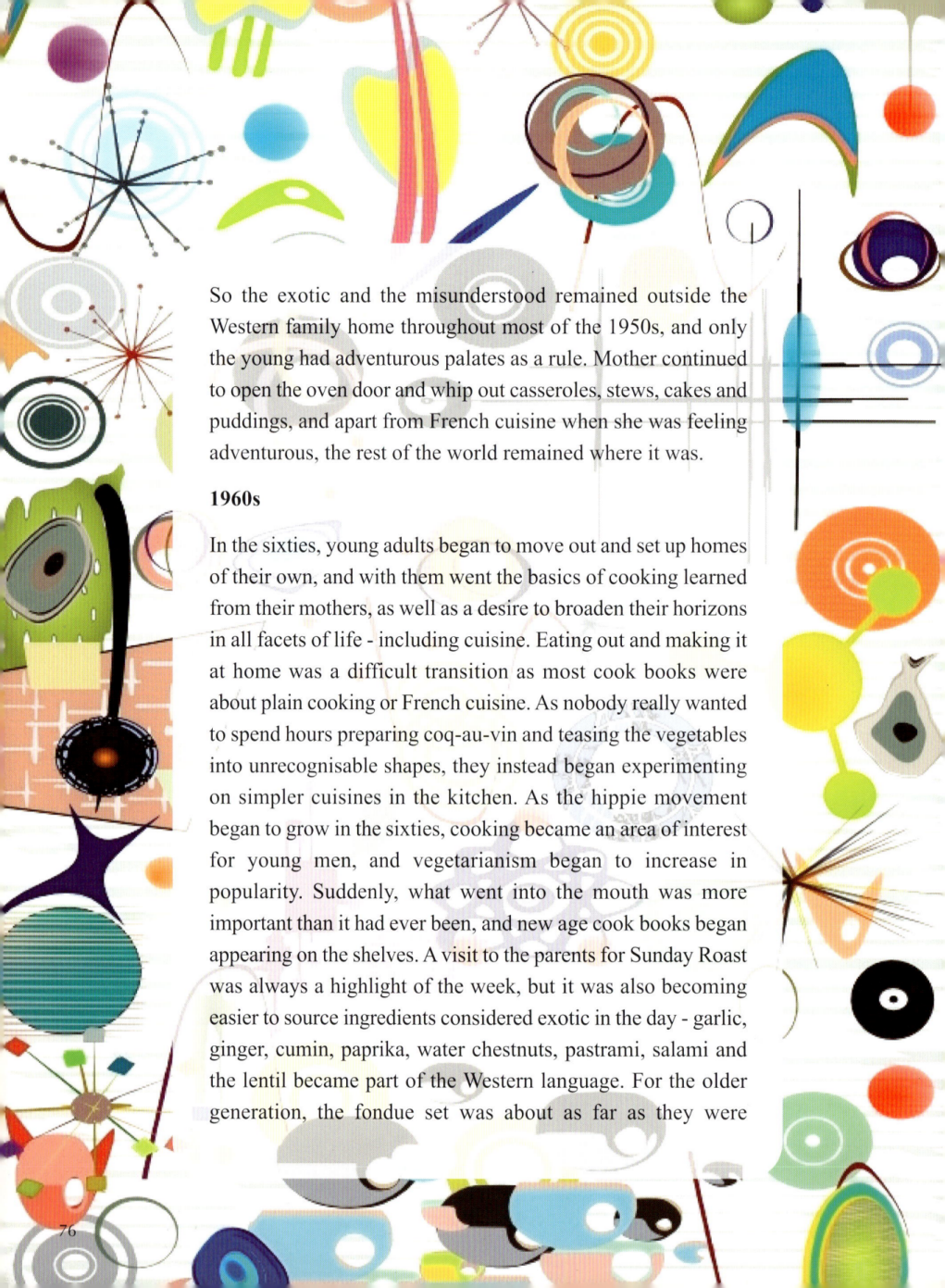

So the exotic and the misunderstood remained outside the Western family home throughout most of the 1950s, and only the young had adventurous palates as a rule. Mother continued to open the oven door and whip out casseroles, stews, cakes and puddings, and apart from French cuisine when she was feeling adventurous, the rest of the world remained where it was.

1960s

In the sixties, young adults began to move out and set up homes of their own, and with them went the basics of cooking learned from their mothers, as well as a desire to broaden their horizons in all facets of life - including cuisine. Eating out and making it at home was a difficult transition as most cook books were about plain cooking or French cuisine. As nobody really wanted to spend hours preparing coq-au-vin and teasing the vegetables into unrecognisable shapes, they instead began experimenting on simpler cuisines in the kitchen. As the hippie movement began to grow in the sixties, cooking became an area of interest for young men, and vegetarianism began to increase in popularity. Suddenly, what went into the mouth was more important than it had ever been, and new age cook books began appearing on the shelves. A visit to the parents for Sunday Roast was always a highlight of the week, but it was also becoming easier to source ingredients considered exotic in the day - garlic, ginger, cumin, paprika, water chestnuts, pastrami, salami and the lentil became part of the Western language. For the older generation, the fondue set was about as far as they were

prepared to go to change the cooking habits of a lifetime, but the young continued experimenting. By the time the troops had returned home from wars in Asia, the demand for a more exotic menu was increasing. Hippies began cooking all sorts of vegetable based concoctions, much of which was based on African cuisine, while second-generation immigrants began to marry outside of their traditional groups and diet changed in accordance with who was at the culinary helm. Italian cuisine mingled with American, while Indian food made the British palate sit up and take note and people everywhere began to learn more about cooking outside the bounds of their own cultural restrictions.

It would be some time before the wok was introduced into the home as an adjunct to the saucepan cupboard, but what came out of the kitchen was changing during the sixties. By the end of the decade *Alice's Restaurant* had shown the world that hippies could cook some pretty appetising meals, and cooking shows had been established on TV. Soon, a woman was able to stand in her kitchen, tune into a cooking show on a small black-and-white set, and be guided step-by-step in the creation of her next great meal. The world was changing everywhere, and the kitchen was a reflection of those times in the late sixties.

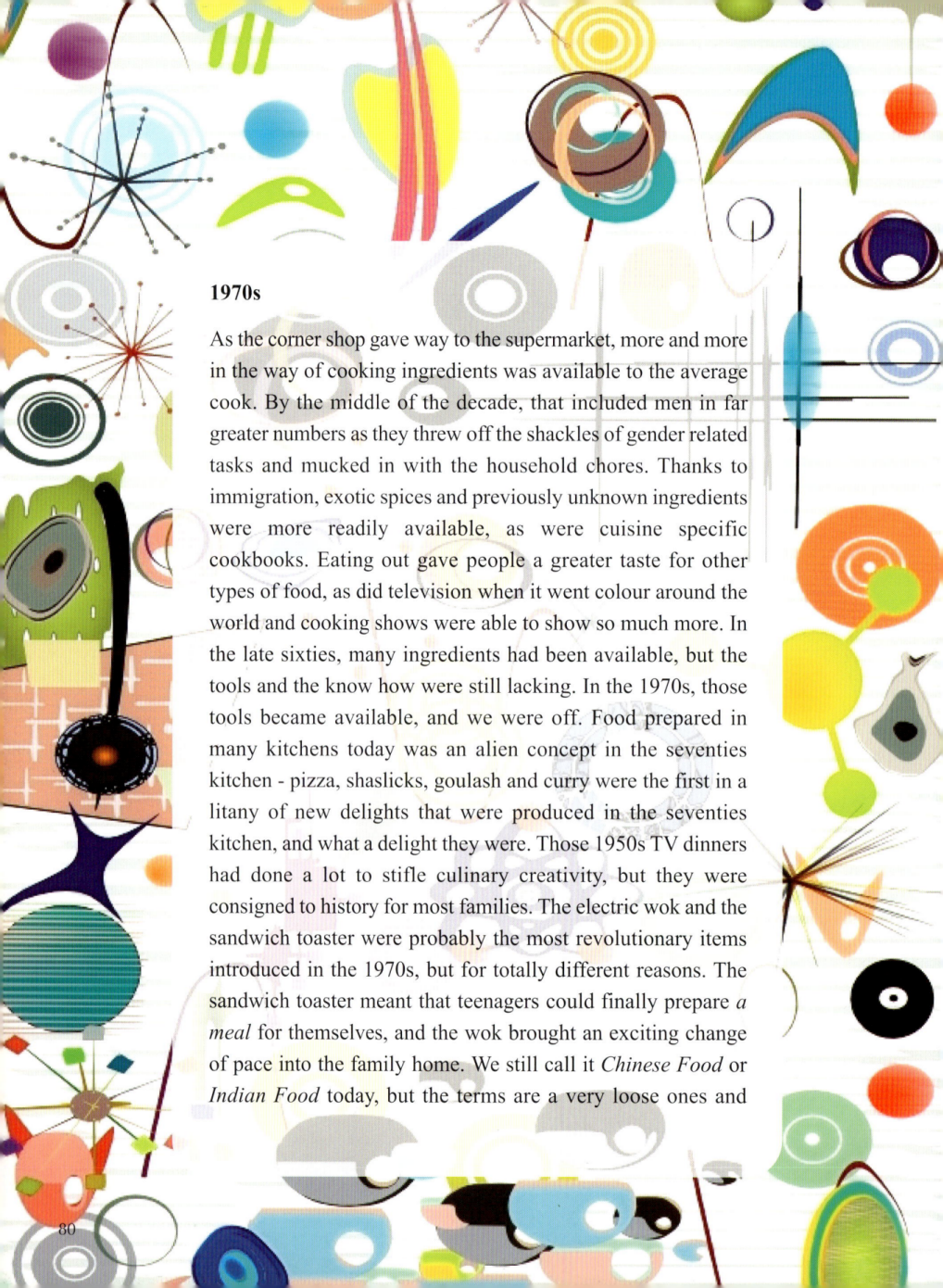

1970s

As the corner shop gave way to the supermarket, more and more in the way of cooking ingredients was available to the average cook. By the middle of the decade, that included men in far greater numbers as they threw off the shackles of gender related tasks and mucked in with the household chores. Thanks to immigration, exotic spices and previously unknown ingredients were more readily available, as were cuisine specific cookbooks. Eating out gave people a greater taste for other types of food, as did television when it went colour around the world and cooking shows were able to show so much more. In the late sixties, many ingredients had been available, but the tools and the know how were still lacking. In the 1970s, those tools became available, and we were off. Food prepared in many kitchens today was an alien concept in the seventies kitchen - pizza, shaslicks, goulash and curry were the first in a litany of new delights that were produced in the seventies kitchen, and what a delight they were. Those 1950s TV dinners had done a lot to stifle culinary creativity, but they were consigned to history for most families. The electric wok and the sandwich toaster were probably the most revolutionary items introduced in the 1970s, but for totally different reasons. The sandwich toaster meant that teenagers could finally prepare *a meal* for themselves, and the wok brought an exciting change of pace into the family home. We still call it *Chinese Food* or *Indian Food* today, but the terms are a very loose ones and

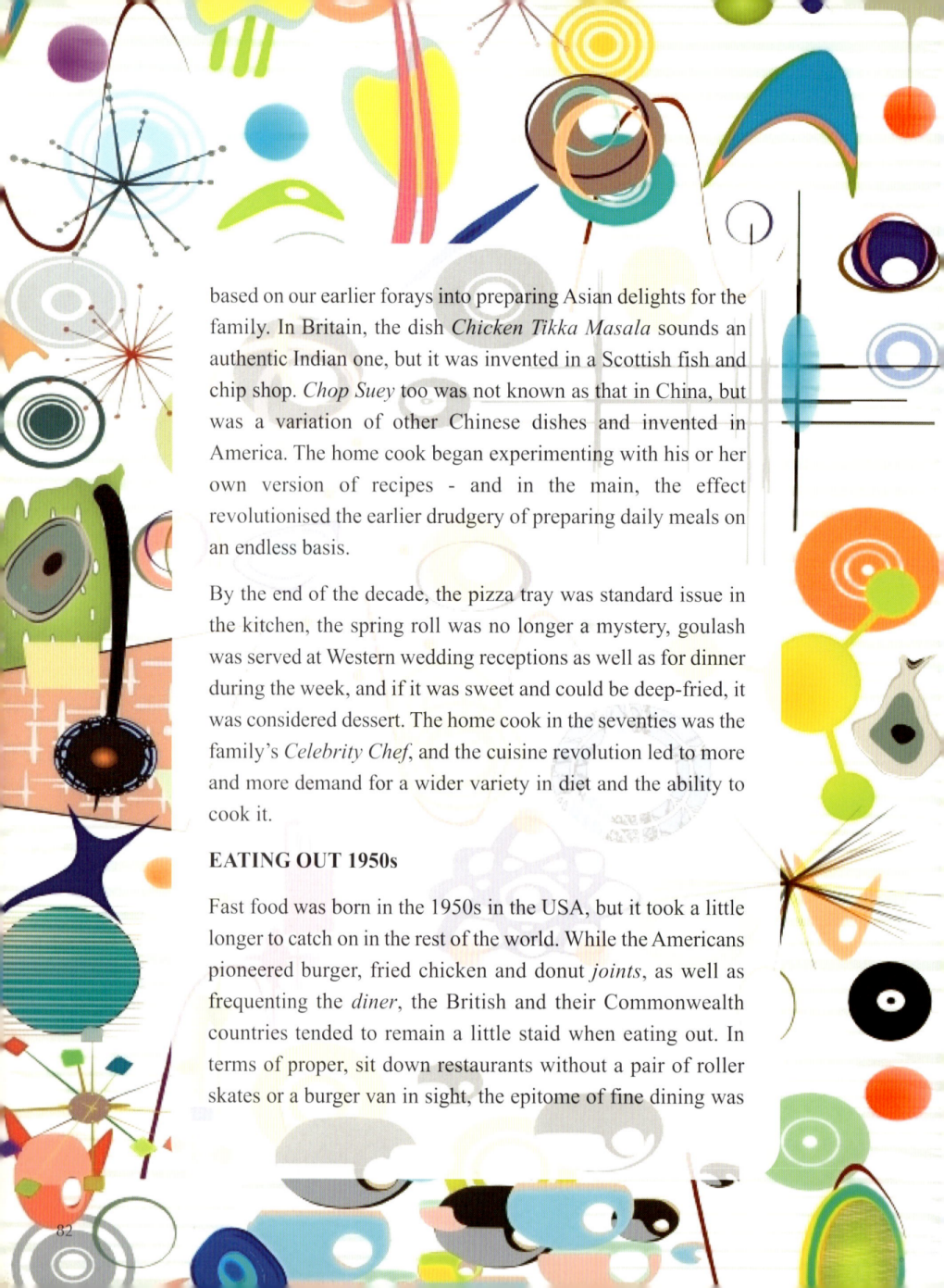

based on our earlier forays into preparing Asian delights for the family. In Britain, the dish *Chicken Tikka Masala* sounds an authentic Indian one, but it was invented in a Scottish fish and chip shop. *Chop Suey* too was not known as that in China, but was a variation of other Chinese dishes and invented in America. The home cook began experimenting with his or her own version of recipes - and in the main, the effect revolutionised the earlier drudgery of preparing daily meals on an endless basis.

By the end of the decade, the pizza tray was standard issue in the kitchen, the spring roll was no longer a mystery, goulash was served at Western wedding receptions as well as for dinner during the week, and if it was sweet and could be deep-fried, it was considered dessert. The home cook in the seventies was the family's *Celebrity Chef*, and the cuisine revolution led to more and more demand for a wider variety in diet and the ability to cook it.

EATING OUT 1950s

Fast food was born in the 1950s in the USA, but it took a little longer to catch on in the rest of the world. While the Americans pioneered burger, fried chicken and donut *joints*, as well as frequenting the *diner*, the British and their Commonwealth countries tended to remain a little staid when eating out. In terms of proper, sit down restaurants without a pair of roller skates or a burger van in sight, the epitome of fine dining was

in a French Restaurant, and many people recognised French cuisine as the best in the world. Meanwhile, back in the real world, families went to family restaurants, and in the 1950s, they were pizza parlours, steak houses and spaghetti joints - busy, fast paced and exciting. A little down the scale were the diners or roadside cafés, followed by hotels with separate dining rooms. If it was a *take-home* meal the family wanted, nothing beat the fish and chip shop, and generations of children were raised on a diet that included at least one meal of fish and chips in the week (generally on pay day). In the USA, it was a burger from the local burger joint, which included the very first *McDonald's Restaurant*. Tens of thousands of Indians arrived in Britain in the late 1940s and early 1950s, and they set up their own restaurants and began changing the British cuisine in perpetuity. Elsewhere in the world, a country's proximity to places such as South America, Asia or Africa dictated who arrived and set up shop. One of the most prolific of cuisines throughout the 20th century was Chinese, and there was generally a Chinese restaurant within a short drive of most people. Of course, for a bit of lunch on the go no matter where you lived, the old stalwart that had been around since World War II was the hot dog, and it remains a favourite today.

1960s

Outside of America, fast food was not the burger joint or the local fried chicken outlet at the beginning of the decade, so not much changed in terms of where food was purchased. But as the sixties drew to a close, there was greater range of cuisine of offer - especially at restaurants. When travelling, the service station began to offer a dine-in facility at restaurants that had initially serviced long distance truck drivers. Realising the benefits of having a captive audience, fuel companies built countrywide chains of service-station restaurants, and the public loved them. Department stores also began offering dining experiences for the midday meal, and many were huge affairs that opened in time for morning tea and closed in the middle of the afternoon. Workers across the city generally flocked to these self-service restaurants, which also had cloak room facilities, telephone booths and areas in which shoppers could rest in armchairs or write at desks that sat along walls. For many travelling salespeople, the department store restaurant was also the office, and was an important centre. Most family restaurants began introducing international dishes into their menus in the sixties as a means of attracting returning customers, while the French Restaurant remained at the top of the blue ribbon dining experience. As the decade drew to a close, the counter culture revolution saw the advent of the health food store and associated eateries. Suddenly, the young began demanding goats milk and vegetarian dishes, and many such businesses

popped up overnight to satisfy a need to eat *naturally*. Customers were often barefoot and tried their hardest to be *windswept and interesting* as they sucked on coconut and banana goat's milk smoothies and munched sesame and wheat germ bars. Naturally, this was totally at odds with the pies and sausage rolls offered at the corner store, or the burgeoning popularity of the *Kentucky Fried Chicken*, *McDonalds* and *Burger King* franchises that were opening up all over the USA and beginning to infiltrate Britain and many other Western countries.

1970s

By the 1970s, there was a huge divide between eating-out experiences. The hippie and student activist culture saw an enormous rise in multicultural eateries centred around natural and vegetarian diets (including the rise in popularity of *soul food* restaurants), while the mainstream were fast embracing the rising numbers of pizza shops and fast food restaurants. Sadly, much of that meant the demise of the diners and cafés that had proliferated for over half a century. Families and singles were busier than ever in the 1970s, and women too had careers, meaning that the preparation of the family meal was no longer the domain of one partner in a relationship. Eating out thus became the solution, and families headed for restaurants at least once a week. The great divide between fast food and traditional food began to widen during the decade. The burgers served at *McDonalds* were totally different to those created at

fish and chip shops and cafés, while *Colonel Sanders* gave the world permission to forego centuries of etiquette and eat fried chicken with their fingers. The steak house was also rising in popularity during the decade, and many were rustically themed to create an atmosphere of eating food that was fresh from the country. Another interesting and fast growing aspect to dining was *dinner theatre*, which came in a number of forms. Some restaurants and theatres offered packages that involved eating at a specific restaurant and then heading straight to the theatre for a show, while others brought the theatre into the restaurant for a themed night. Whatever was on the stage was replicated on the plate, and such venues were very popular into the 1980s and beyond. Roman, Medieval and Hawaiian nights were the most popular, and the working classes lapped it up as a wonderful escape from everyday life.

IN THE WORKPLACE

BLUE COLLAR

In the 1950s, what your parents and grandparents did had a huge impact upon what you did for a living. Unless you were some form of genius and in possession of scholarship with all expenses paid, there was little expectation of moving outside of the traditional family profession. The only exception to the rule was in the scholarships available to the children of the war dead in Commonwealth countries, who were eligible for scholarships providing they were of a certain scholastic level. For the rest of the world, it was far more simple. A man who worked as a miner, a boilermaker or a chef often managed to find a job for his son working alongside or near him. Nepotism meant that the children of factory workers often had an advantage in getting into a company as employees, and that included labouring women as well as men. If you owned a shop or a restaurant, the family often worked alongside you anyway, and it was just a matter of handing over the reins when ill health or retirement loomed.

An apprenticeship was a great thing to have in a working class family in the 20th century. Apprenticeships led to qualifications in plumbing, carpentry, metal trades and mechanics, and were often used as a stepping stone into independent business ownership later in life. All the way from the 1950s into the 1980s, most tradesmen (there were very few women) wore the

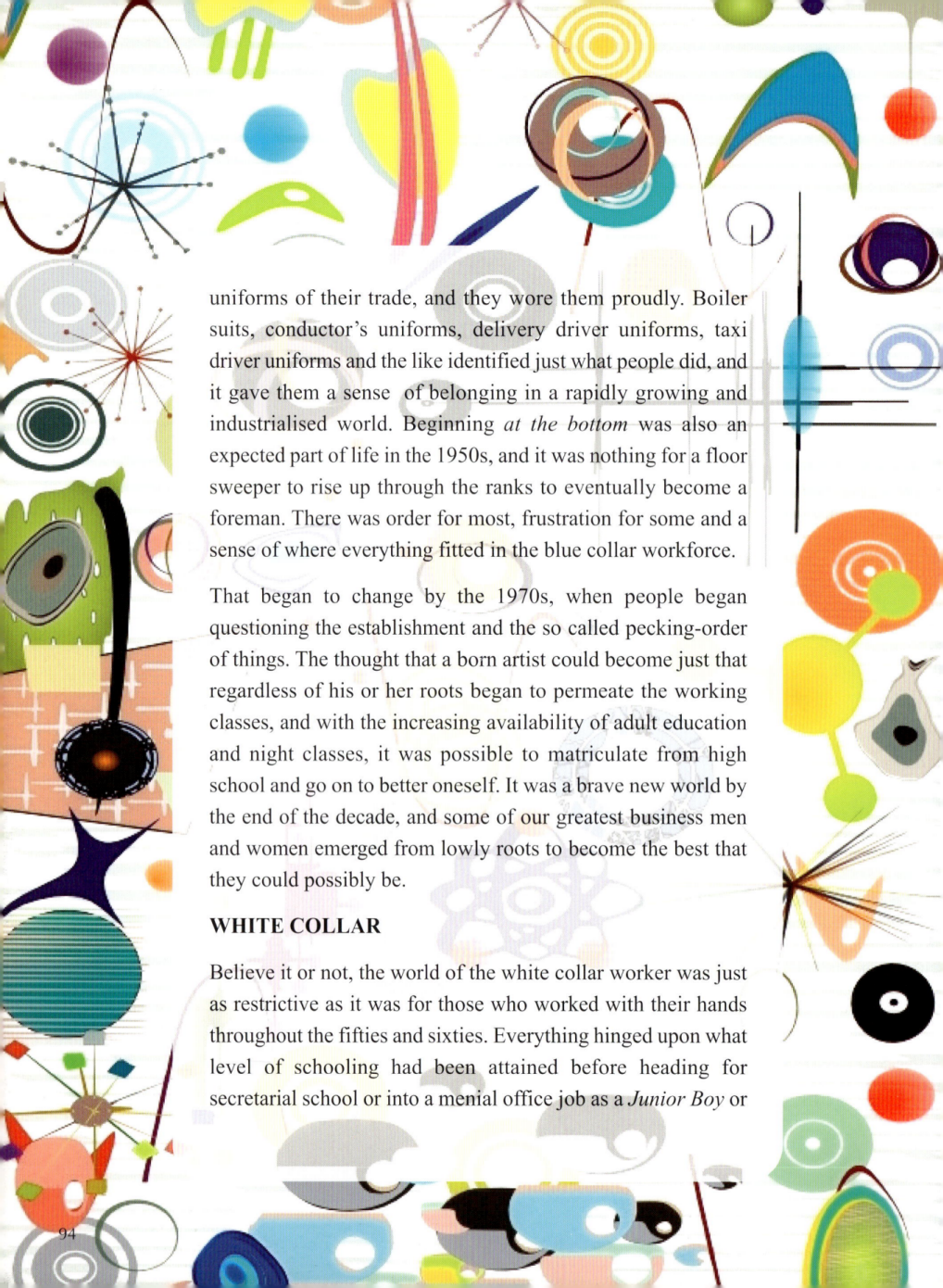

uniforms of their trade, and they wore them proudly. Boiler suits, conductor's uniforms, delivery driver uniforms, taxi driver uniforms and the like identified just what people did, and it gave them a sense of belonging in a rapidly growing and industrialised world. Beginning *at the bottom* was also an expected part of life in the 1950s, and it was nothing for a floor sweeper to rise up through the ranks to eventually become a foreman. There was order for most, frustration for some and a sense of where everything fitted in the blue collar workforce.

That began to change by the 1970s, when people began questioning the establishment and the so called pecking-order of things. The thought that a born artist could become just that regardless of his or her roots began to permeate the working classes, and with the increasing availability of adult education and night classes, it was possible to matriculate from high school and go on to better oneself. It was a brave new world by the end of the decade, and some of our greatest business men and women emerged from lowly roots to become the best that they could possibly be.

WHITE COLLAR

Believe it or not, the world of the white collar worker was just as restrictive as it was for those who worked with their hands throughout the fifties and sixties. Everything hinged upon what level of schooling had been attained before heading for secretarial school or into a menial office job as a *Junior Boy* or

a *Girl Friday*. For the girl who attended secretarial college, she was generally recruited straight out of the college and landed up in the typing pool of a large government or private firm. In the 1950s, marriage meant dismissal, and as most women were expected to marry and have children, there was little to be gained in trying to advance. The young man who began in the mail room was different. It was expected that he would eventually work his way up into a clerical position that had him filing documents, and he was encouraged to head for night school to learn book keeping or accounting.

Professional people who worked in offices were accountants, lawyers, engineers, architects and the like, and it was their job to run companies, which in turn ran the world. Reaching an executive position was generally only achieved by lawyers and engineers (who were imbued with special powers), and moving between jobs was frowned upon. In the 1960s, there was far more scope for a professional to move about, and many companies began head hunting people they wanted on their team. In the lower ranks of administration, jobs were fairly thick on the ground, and good secretaries could go places if they chose the right company. Women also operated complex adding machines and were considered the ideal candidate for researching and compiling other peoples' work, but there was still a general bias against a colleague who others knew would one day down tools to become a mother. By the end of the 1970s, women were choosing to continue with their careers

after a few years out to raise children to school age, and it was not unusual for men and women alike to believe that they had a *job for life* - but that was about to change when the first of economic downturns happened in the 1980s.

PROFESSIONAL AND SERVICE INDUSTRIES

The main service areas in the 1950s were the police forces, the ambulance or fire services, the armed forces, the nursing profession or in hospitality. Each was reasonably lowly paid between the 1950s and the 1970s, and most had fairly strict entry requirements. For women, most of the services only took men, and in those that did employ women, the entry age was 21. That left two professions for an 18-year-old girl on the cusp of leaving school and wanting to do more than work in a shop or an office - she could become a nurse or an air stewardess. The professionals who the general public were generally in regular contact with were teachers and doctors, and they were well respected within communities.

In the 1950s, policing was a risky business. During World War II, organised crime had been in full swing selling black market goods, and by the war's end, were thick with money and hangers on. Criminal gangs operated in certain areas of cities, and most police officers preferred not to go there as it meant either certain death or being coerced into breaking the law themselves y turning a blind eye. For the average citizen, the police were a comforting sight on the streets, often stationed on every corner and armed with a whistle in case of danger. By the

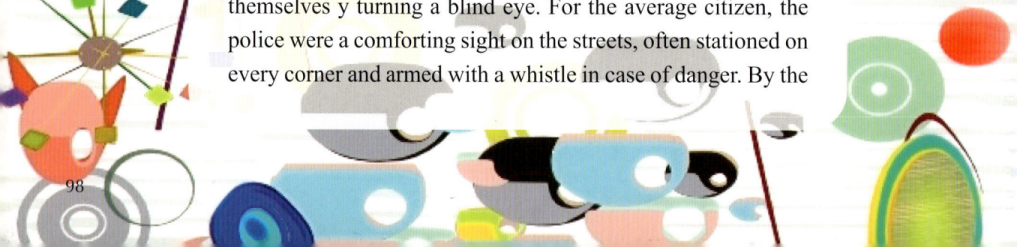

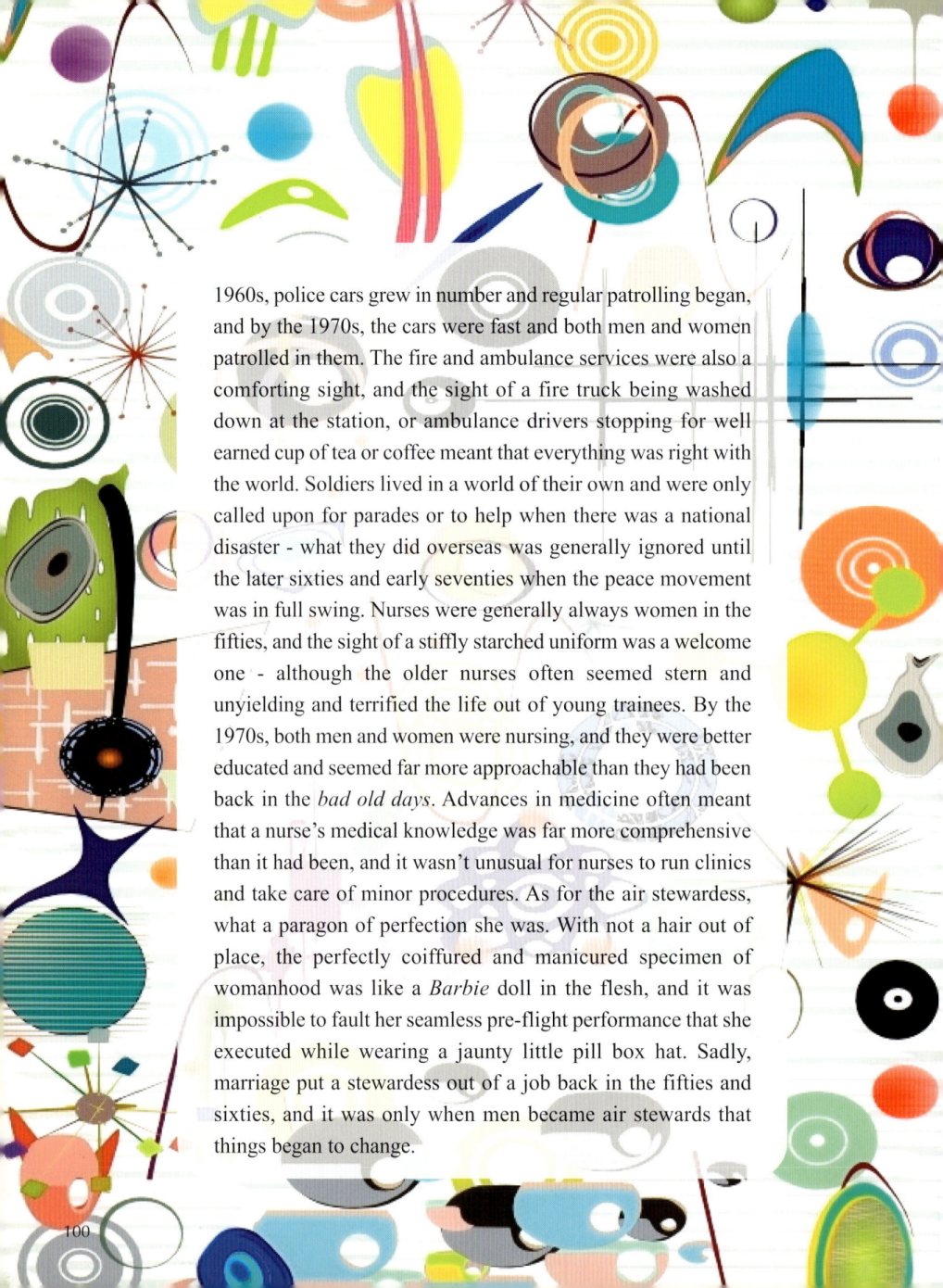

1960s, police cars grew in number and regular patrolling began, and by the 1970s, the cars were fast and both men and women patrolled in them. The fire and ambulance services were also a comforting sight, and the sight of a fire truck being washed down at the station, or ambulance drivers stopping for well earned cup of tea or coffee meant that everything was right with the world. Soldiers lived in a world of their own and were only called upon for parades or to help when there was a national disaster - what they did overseas was generally ignored until the later sixties and early seventies when the peace movement was in full swing. Nurses were generally always women in the fifties, and the sight of a stiffly starched uniform was a welcome one - although the older nurses often seemed stern and unyielding and terrified the life out of young trainees. By the 1970s, both men and women were nursing, and they were better educated and seemed far more approachable than they had been back in the *bad old days*. Advances in medicine often meant that a nurse's medical knowledge was far more comprehensive than it had been, and it wasn't unusual for nurses to run clinics and take care of minor procedures. As for the air stewardess, what a paragon of perfection she was. With not a hair out of place, the perfectly coiffured and manicured specimen of womanhood was like a *Barbie* doll in the flesh, and it was impossible to fault her seamless pre-flight performance that she executed while wearing a jaunty little pill box hat. Sadly, marriage put a stewardess out of a job back in the fifties and sixties, and it was only when men became air stewards that things began to change.

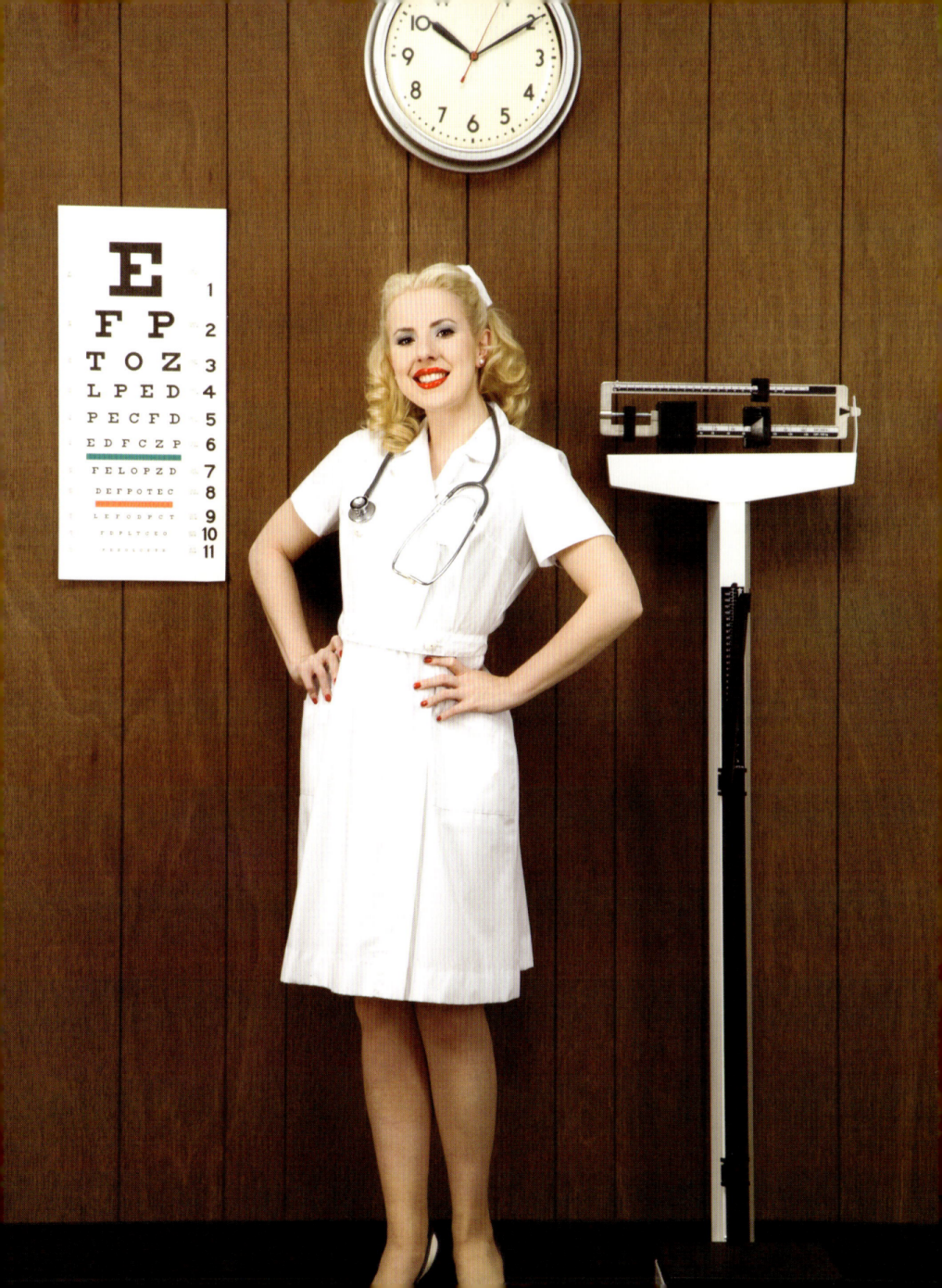

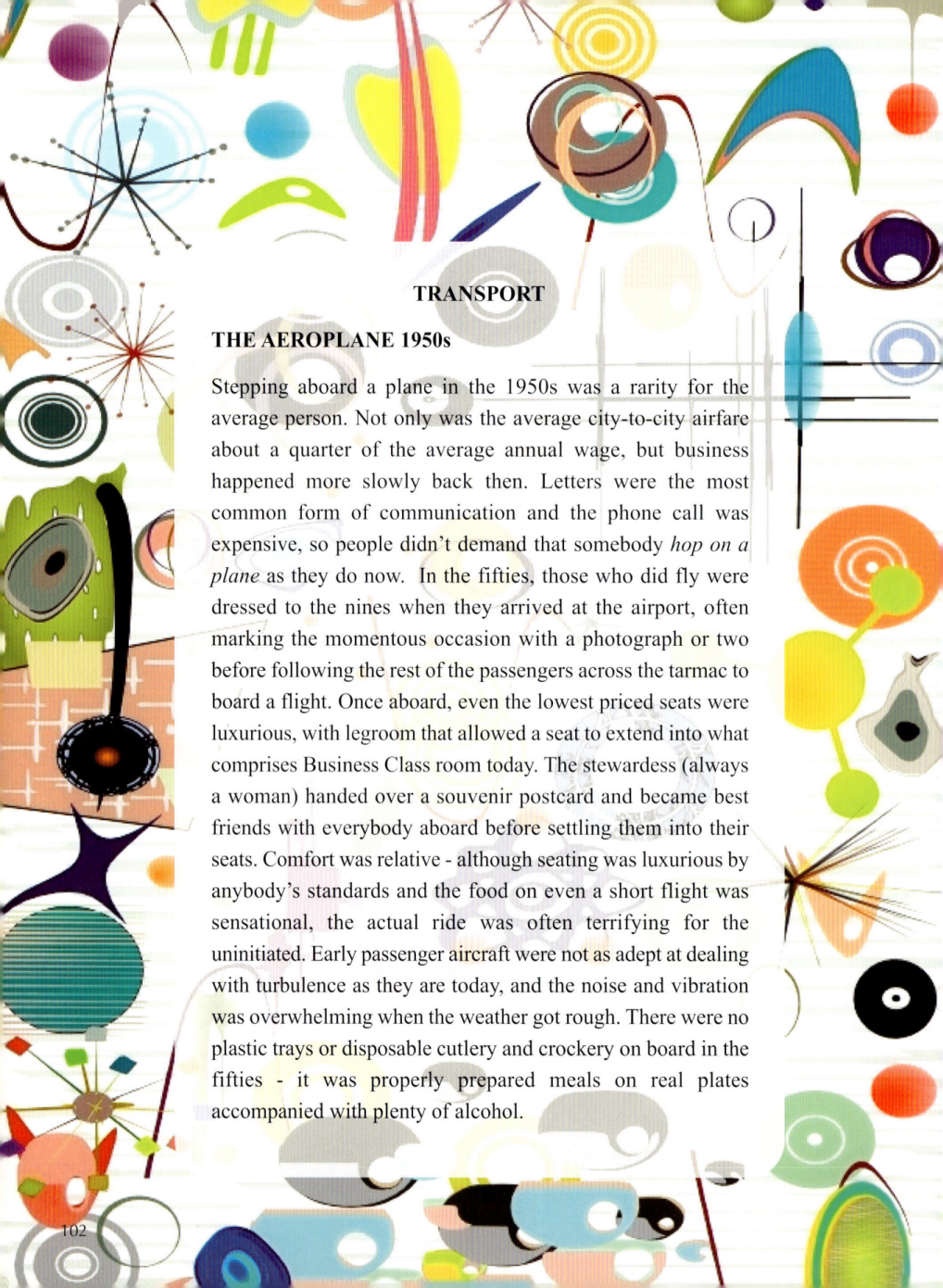

TRANSPORT

THE AEROPLANE 1950s

Stepping aboard a plane in the 1950s was a rarity for the average person. Not only was the average city-to-city airfare about a quarter of the average annual wage, but business happened more slowly back then. Letters were the most common form of communication and the phone call was expensive, so people didn't demand that somebody *hop on a plane* as they do now. In the fifties, those who did fly were dressed to the nines when they arrived at the airport, often marking the momentous occasion with a photograph or two before following the rest of the passengers across the tarmac to board a flight. Once aboard, even the lowest priced seats were luxurious, with legroom that allowed a seat to extend into what comprises Business Class room today. The stewardess (always a woman) handed over a souvenir postcard and became best friends with everybody aboard before settling them into their seats. Comfort was relative - although seating was luxurious by anybody's standards and the food on even a short flight was sensational, the actual ride was often terrifying for the uninitiated. Early passenger aircraft were not as adept at dealing with turbulence as they are today, and the noise and vibration was overwhelming when the weather got rough. There were no plastic trays or disposable cutlery and crockery on board in the fifties - it was properly prepared meals on real plates accompanied with plenty of alcohol.

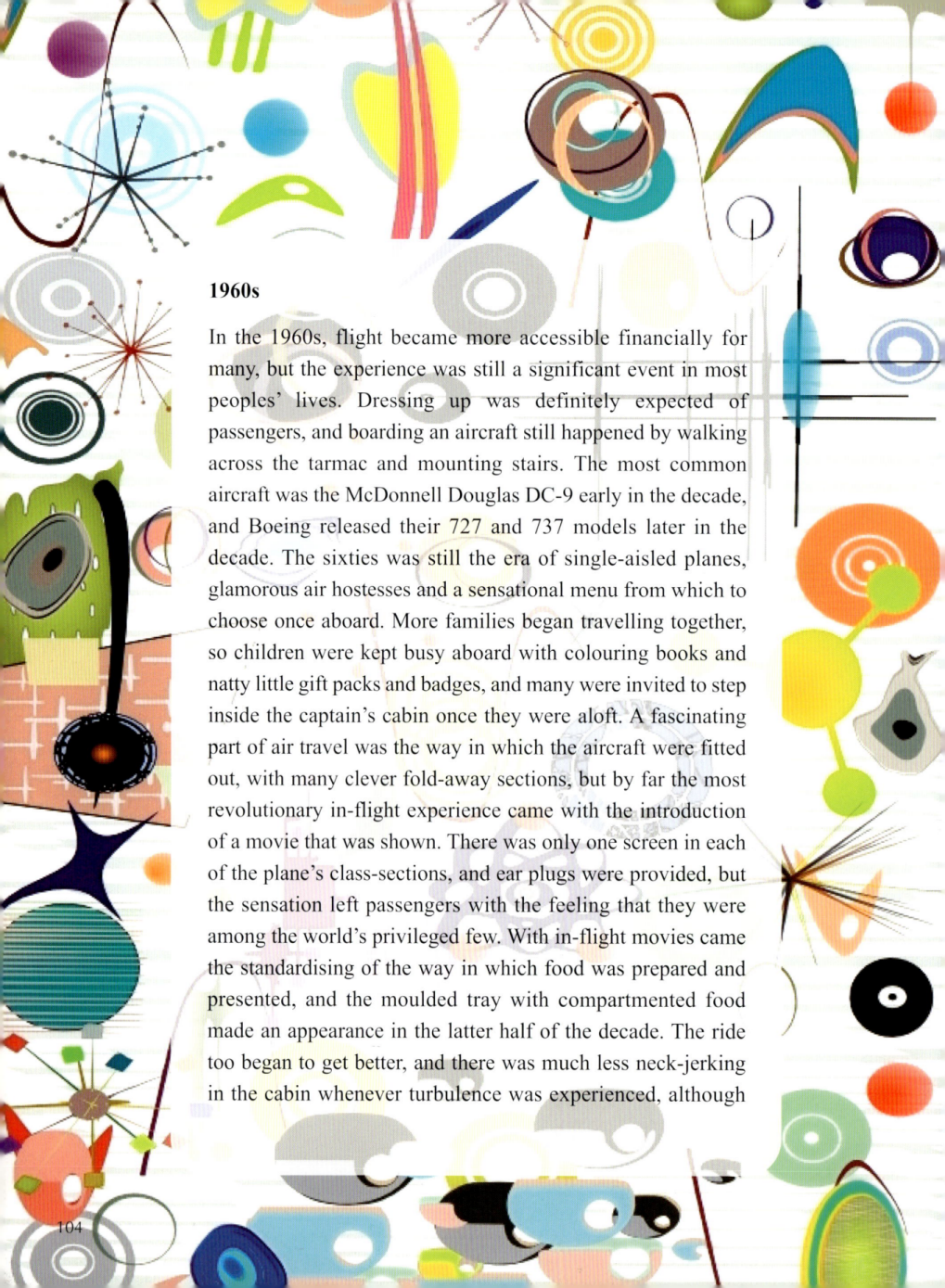

1960s

In the 1960s, flight became more accessible financially for many, but the experience was still a significant event in most peoples' lives. Dressing up was definitely expected of passengers, and boarding an aircraft still happened by walking across the tarmac and mounting stairs. The most common aircraft was the McDonnell Douglas DC-9 early in the decade, and Boeing released their 727 and 737 models later in the decade. The sixties was still the era of single-aisled planes, glamorous air hostesses and a sensational menu from which to choose once aboard. More families began travelling together, so children were kept busy aboard with colouring books and natty little gift packs and badges, and many were invited to step inside the captain's cabin once they were aloft. A fascinating part of air travel was the way in which the aircraft were fitted out, with many clever fold-away sections, but by far the most revolutionary in-flight experience came with the introduction of a movie that was shown. There was only one screen in each of the plane's class-sections, and ear plugs were provided, but the sensation left passengers with the feeling that they were among the world's privileged few. With in-flight movies came the standardising of the way in which food was prepared and presented, and the moulded tray with compartmented food made an appearance in the latter half of the decade. The ride too began to get better, and there was much less neck-jerking in the cabin whenever turbulence was experienced, although

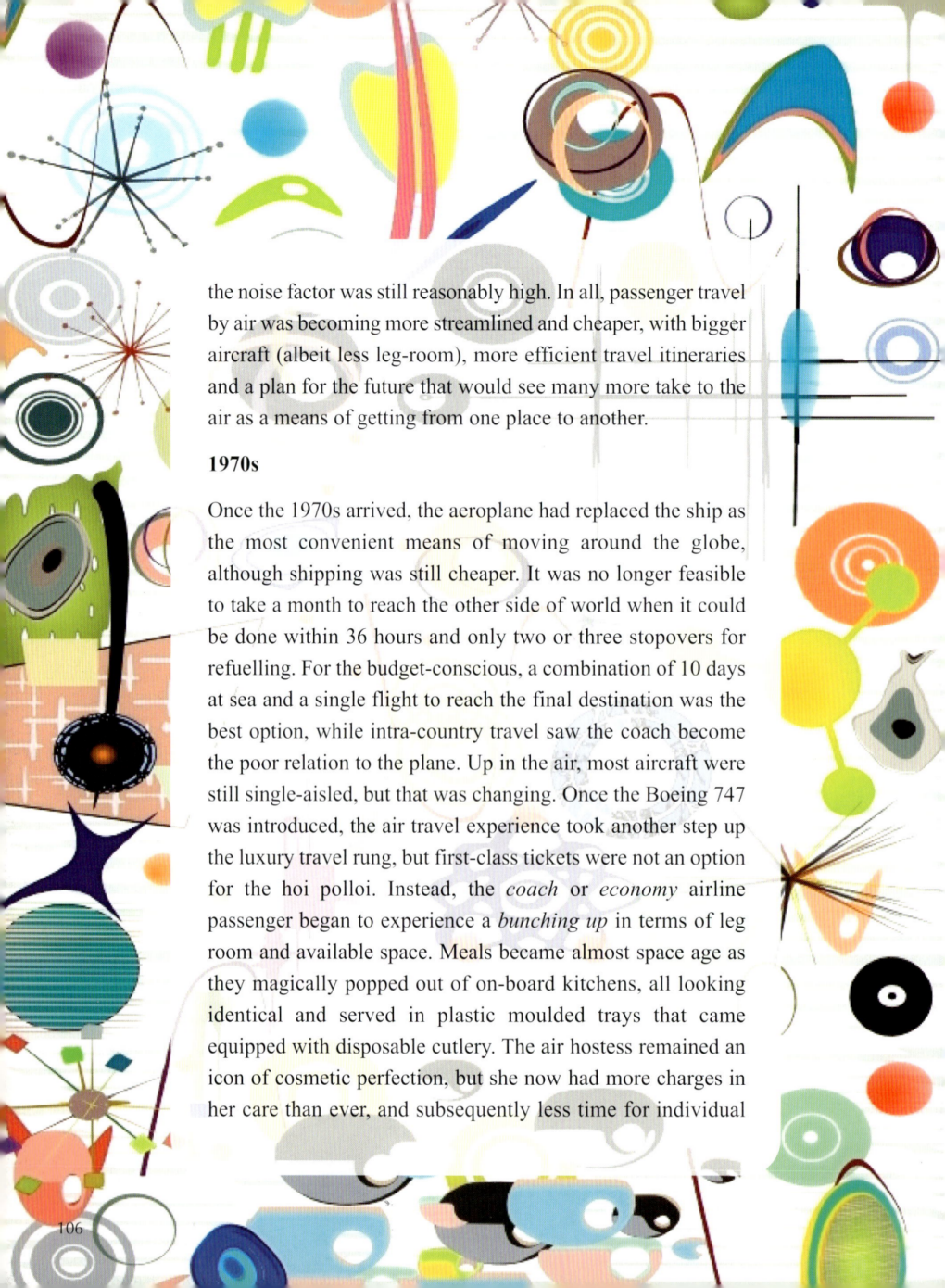

the noise factor was still reasonably high. In all, passenger travel by air was becoming more streamlined and cheaper, with bigger aircraft (albeit less leg-room), more efficient travel itineraries and a plan for the future that would see many more take to the air as a means of getting from one place to another.

1970s

Once the 1970s arrived, the aeroplane had replaced the ship as the most convenient means of moving around the globe, although shipping was still cheaper. It was no longer feasible to take a month to reach the other side of world when it could be done within 36 hours and only two or three stopovers for refuelling. For the budget-conscious, a combination of 10 days at sea and a single flight to reach the final destination was the best option, while intra-country travel saw the coach become the poor relation to the plane. Up in the air, most aircraft were still single-aisled, but that was changing. Once the Boeing 747 was introduced, the air travel experience took another step up the luxury travel rung, but first-class tickets were not an option for the hoi polloi. Instead, the *coach* or *economy* airline passenger began to experience a *bunching up* in terms of leg room and available space. Meals became almost space age as they magically popped out of on-board kitchens, all looking identical and served in plastic moulded trays that came equipped with disposable cutlery. The air hostess remained an icon of cosmetic perfection, but she now had more charges in her care than ever, and subsequently less time for individual

bonding. In-flight entertainment was generally a movie shown on a single screen, and airlines began charging passengers for the privilege of listening (ear phones were sold). Extras such as alcohol and snacks were also paid for, and the only thing free were the slippers handed out on international flights. As with anything that was mass produced in the 1970s, the price to pay for flight available to the masses was a homogenisation of the on-board experience. Nevertheless, flying in the 1970s was still quite an adventure, and many a wonderful memories remains of the last decade of the *golden age* of air travel.

THE CAR 1950s

If a family (or a single person) could afford a car in the 1950s, the early years of the decade had a lot in second-hand autos available, as well as a growing number of shiny new models in colours other than black. The roads began to fill with cars that were all so different from each other, in a time when badge engineering wasn't even thought of by most. British and American cars were the most popular, while French and German cars also found their way around the world. By the end of the decade, Japanese cars also came onto the market, but they weren't a patch on what they would become. From England came the smaller family cars made by companies such as Morris, Austin, Vauxhall and Hillman, while larger and more luxurious cars had the names of Jaguar, Rolls Royce and Bentley on their badges. The British car industry was huge at the time, and some of the country's most iconic motors were

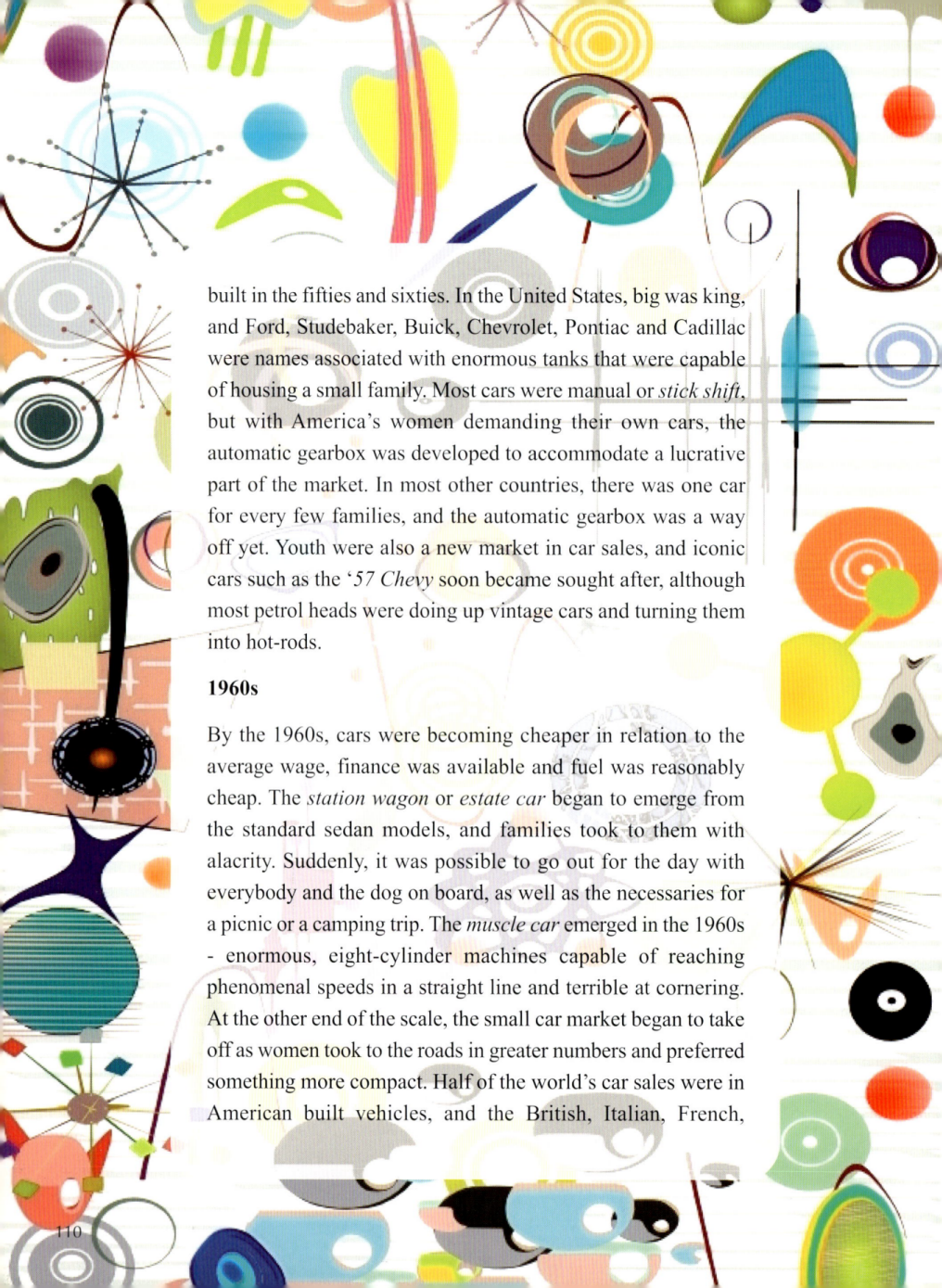

built in the fifties and sixties. In the United States, big was king, and Ford, Studebaker, Buick, Chevrolet, Pontiac and Cadillac were names associated with enormous tanks that were capable of housing a small family. Most cars were manual or *stick shift*, but with America's women demanding their own cars, the automatic gearbox was developed to accommodate a lucrative part of the market. In most other countries, there was one car for every few families, and the automatic gearbox was a way off yet. Youth were also a new market in car sales, and iconic cars such as the *'57 Chevy* soon became sought after, although most petrol heads were doing up vintage cars and turning them into hot-rods.

1960s

By the 1960s, cars were becoming cheaper in relation to the average wage, finance was available and fuel was reasonably cheap. The *station wagon* or *estate car* began to emerge from the standard sedan models, and families took to them with alacrity. Suddenly, it was possible to go out for the day with everybody and the dog on board, as well as the necessaries for a picnic or a camping trip. The *muscle car* emerged in the 1960s - enormous, eight-cylinder machines capable of reaching phenomenal speeds in a straight line and terrible at cornering. At the other end of the scale, the small car market began to take off as women took to the roads in greater numbers and preferred something more compact. Half of the world's car sales were in American built vehicles, and the British, Italian, French,

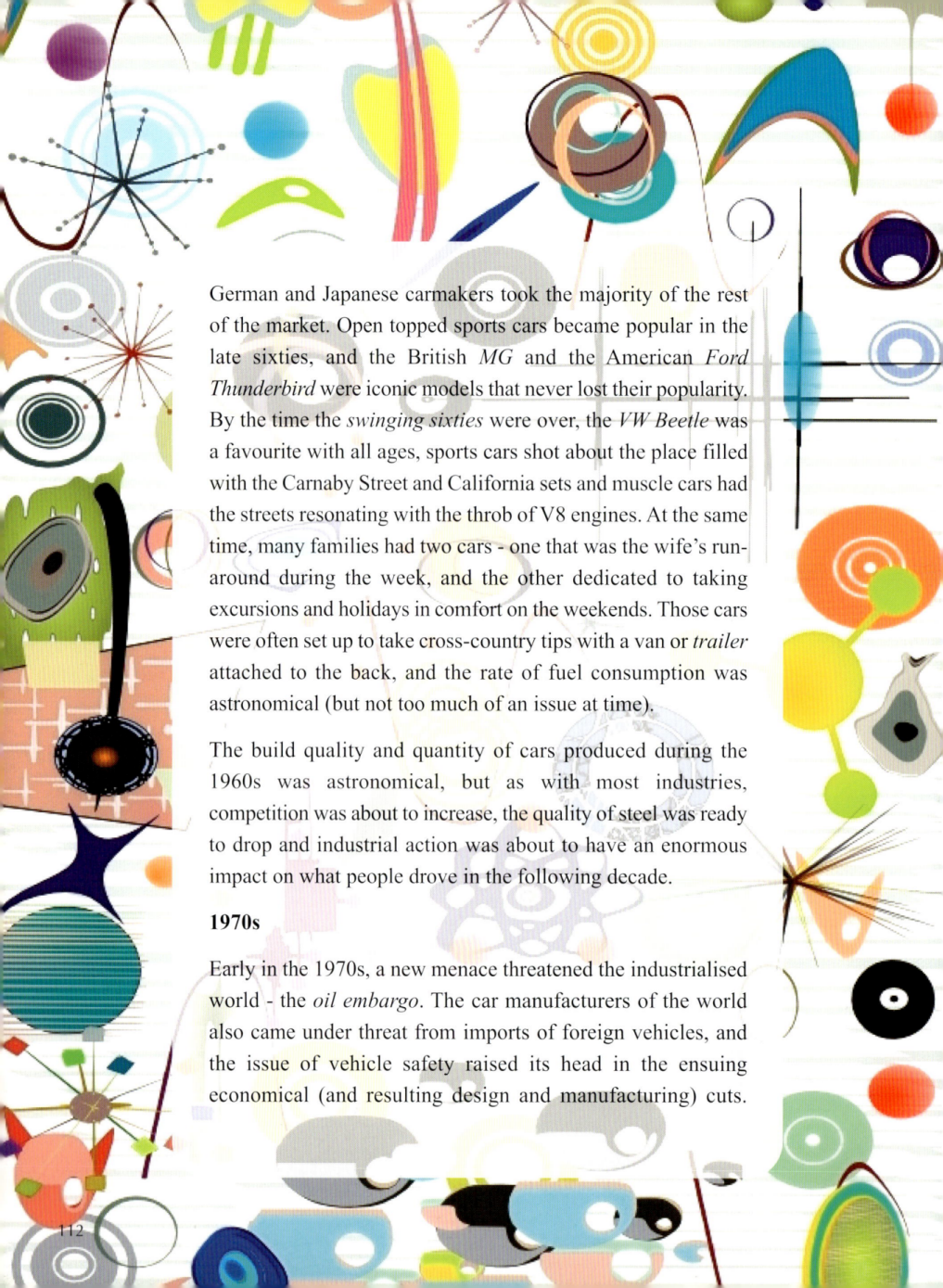

German and Japanese carmakers took the majority of the rest of the market. Open topped sports cars became popular in the late sixties, and the British *MG* and the American *Ford Thunderbird* were iconic models that never lost their popularity. By the time the *swinging sixties* were over, the *VW Beetle* was a favourite with all ages, sports cars shot about the place filled with the Carnaby Street and California sets and muscle cars had the streets resonating with the throb of V8 engines. At the same time, many families had two cars - one that was the wife's run-around during the week, and the other dedicated to taking excursions and holidays in comfort on the weekends. Those cars were often set up to take cross-country tips with a van or *trailer* attached to the back, and the rate of fuel consumption was astronomical (but not too much of an issue at time).

The build quality and quantity of cars produced during the 1960s was astronomical, but as with most industries, competition was about to increase, the quality of steel was ready to drop and industrial action was about to have an enormous impact on what people drove in the following decade.

1970s

Early in the 1970s, a new menace threatened the industrialised world - the *oil embargo*. The car manufacturers of the world also came under threat from imports of foreign vehicles, and the issue of vehicle safety raised its head in the ensuing economical (and resulting design and manufacturing) cuts.

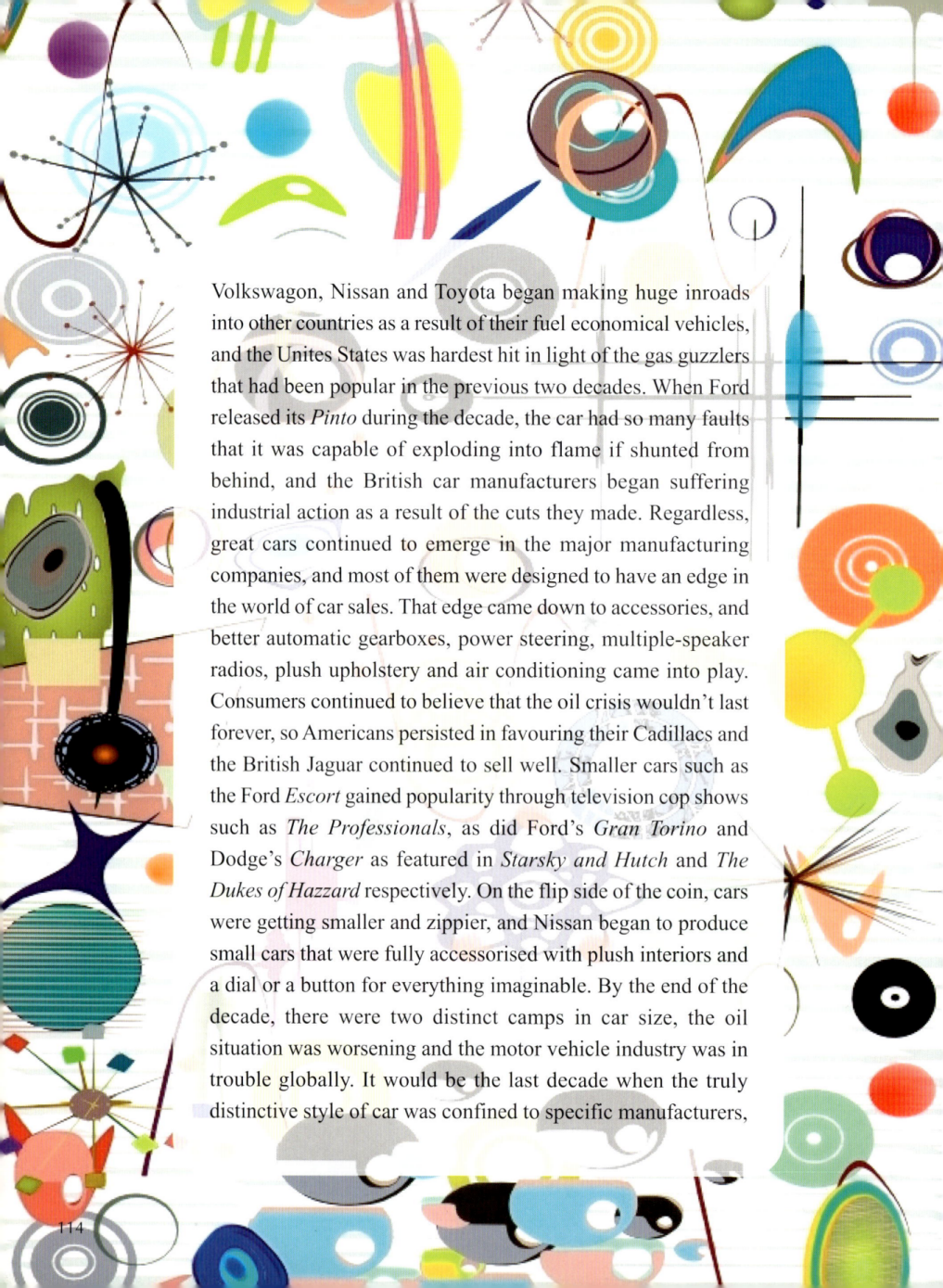

Volkswagon, Nissan and Toyota began making huge inroads into other countries as a result of their fuel economical vehicles, and the Unites States was hardest hit in light of the gas guzzlers that had been popular in the previous two decades. When Ford released its *Pinto* during the decade, the car had so many faults that it was capable of exploding into flame if shunted from behind, and the British car manufacturers began suffering industrial action as a result of the cuts they made. Regardless, great cars continued to emerge in the major manufacturing companies, and most of them were designed to have an edge in the world of car sales. That edge came down to accessories, and better automatic gearboxes, power steering, multiple-speaker radios, plush upholstery and air conditioning came into play. Consumers continued to believe that the oil crisis wouldn't last forever, so Americans persisted in favouring their Cadillacs and the British Jaguar continued to sell well. Smaller cars such as the Ford *Escort* gained popularity through television cop shows such as *The Professionals*, as did Ford's *Gran Torino* and Dodge's *Charger* as featured in *Starsky and Hutch* and *The Dukes of Hazzard* respectively. On the flip side of the coin, cars were getting smaller and zippier, and Nissan began to produce small cars that were fully accessorised with plush interiors and a dial or a button for everything imaginable. By the end of the decade, there were two distinct camps in car size, the oil situation was worsening and the motor vehicle industry was in trouble globally. It would be the last decade when the truly distinctive style of car was confined to specific manufacturers,

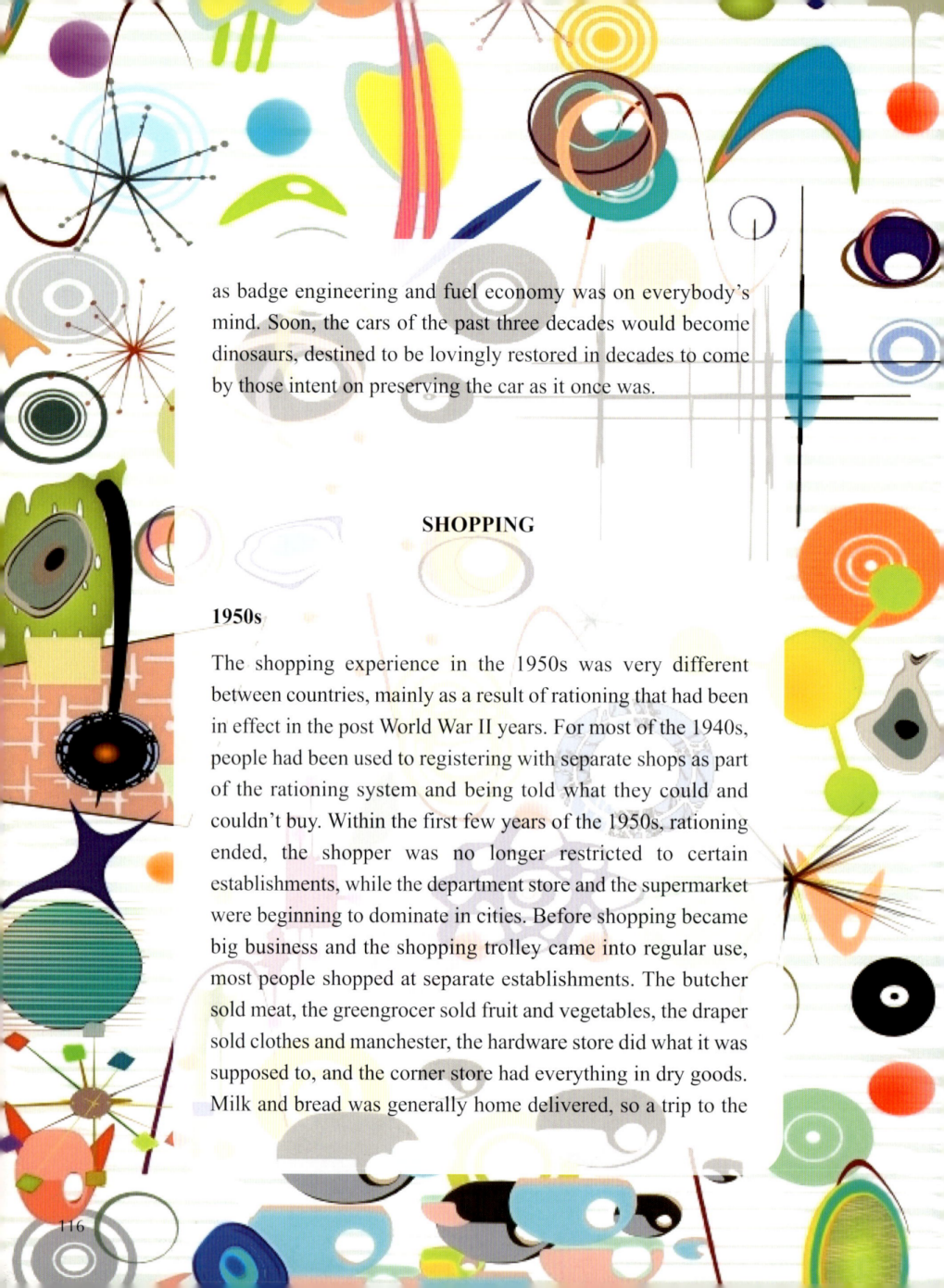

as badge engineering and fuel economy was on everybody's mind. Soon, the cars of the past three decades would become dinosaurs, destined to be lovingly restored in decades to come by those intent on preserving the car as it once was.

SHOPPING

1950s

The shopping experience in the 1950s was very different between countries, mainly as a result of rationing that had been in effect in the post World War II years. For most of the 1940s, people had been used to registering with separate shops as part of the rationing system and being told what they could and couldn't buy. Within the first few years of the 1950s, rationing ended, the shopper was no longer restricted to certain establishments, while the department store and the supermarket were beginning to dominate in cities. Before shopping became big business and the shopping trolley came into regular use, most people shopped at separate establishments. The butcher sold meat, the greengrocer sold fruit and vegetables, the draper sold clothes and manchester, the hardware store did what it was supposed to, and the corner store had everything in dry goods. Milk and bread was generally home delivered, so a trip to the

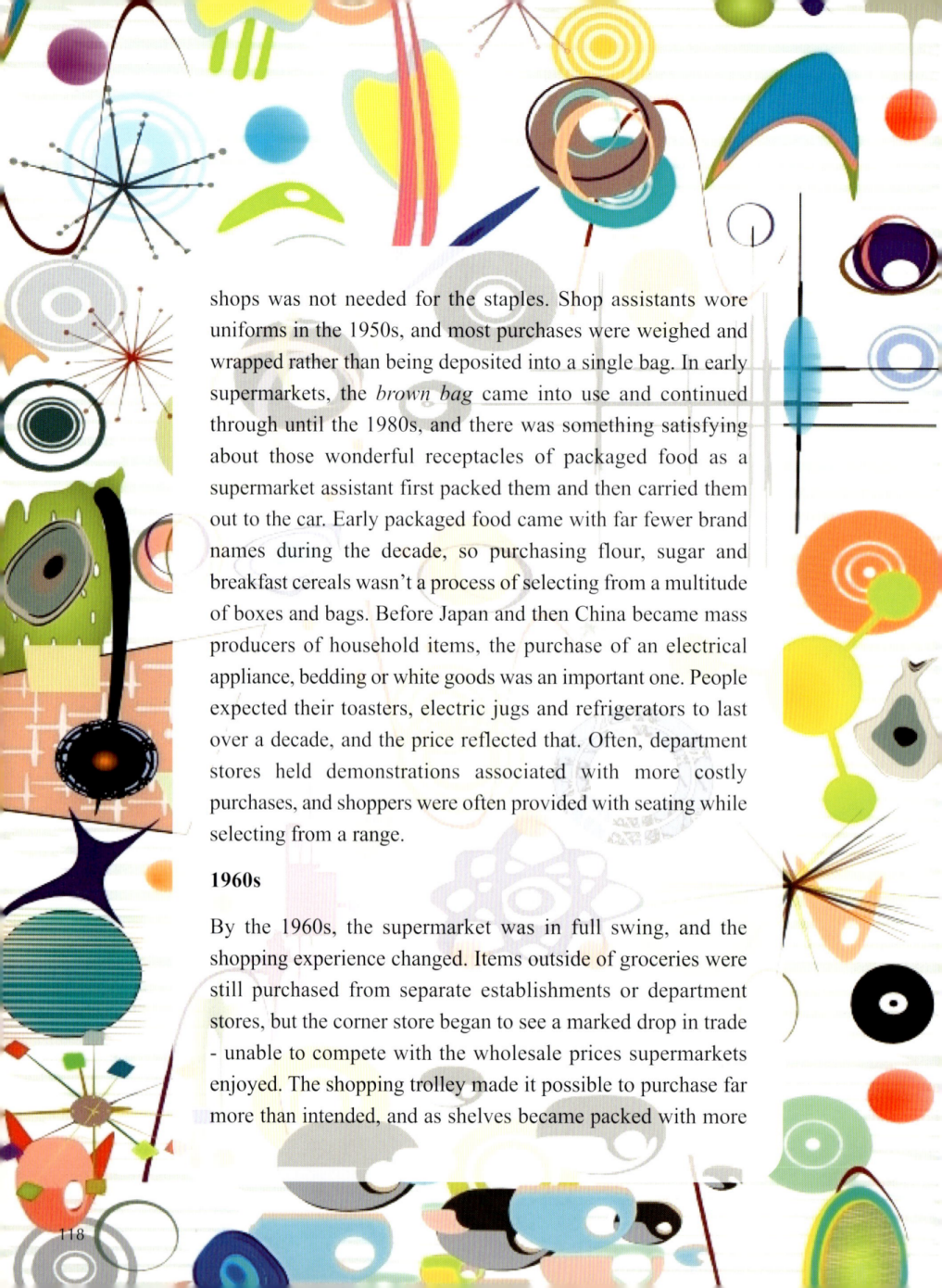

shops was not needed for the staples. Shop assistants wore uniforms in the 1950s, and most purchases were weighed and wrapped rather than being deposited into a single bag. In early supermarkets, the *brown bag* came into use and continued through until the 1980s, and there was something satisfying about those wonderful receptacles of packaged food as a supermarket assistant first packed them and then carried them out to the car. Early packaged food came with far fewer brand names during the decade, so purchasing flour, sugar and breakfast cereals wasn't a process of selecting from a multitude of boxes and bags. Before Japan and then China became mass producers of household items, the purchase of an electrical appliance, bedding or white goods was an important one. People expected their toasters, electric jugs and refrigerators to last over a decade, and the price reflected that. Often, department stores held demonstrations associated with more costly purchases, and shoppers were often provided with seating while selecting from a range.

1960s

By the 1960s, the supermarket was in full swing, and the shopping experience changed. Items outside of groceries were still purchased from separate establishments or department stores, but the corner store began to see a marked drop in trade - unable to compete with the wholesale prices supermarkets enjoyed. The shopping trolley made it possible to purchase far more than intended, and as shelves became packed with more

and more brands, weekly specials and discount coupons began appearing in newspapers and magazines. Suddenly, the family could save quite a bit if it favoured one chain of supermarkets and purchased more than one of a specially marked item, and mental maths acumen was a handy talent to have. As more and more women began driving the family car, so they were able to venture away from the family home on shopping expeditions, and competition became fiercer. This led to the consumer often being the winner in price wars, and the rising popularity of the shopping trip as a social event. Department stores saw the value in promoting the shopping experience as a full day out, and they had large restaurants equipped with cloak rooms, phone booths and rest areas. Shopping for children began to increase as more and more variety came into the market in clothing, shoes and toys, and children began learning how to shop from a young age. In turn, that prompted the addition of ice cream vendors and sweet shops near larger stores, as well as the concept of the shopping mall as a place for families to shop as a whole. By the time the decade ended, the specialty store was part of the indoor or outdoor shopping *centre*, which generally housed more than one popular supermarket chain and at least one department store. Local authorities soon began incorporating shop fronts for administrative services that required the payment of fees, and the teen market also began frequenting record shops and snack bars that set up undercover shops or stalls within centres.

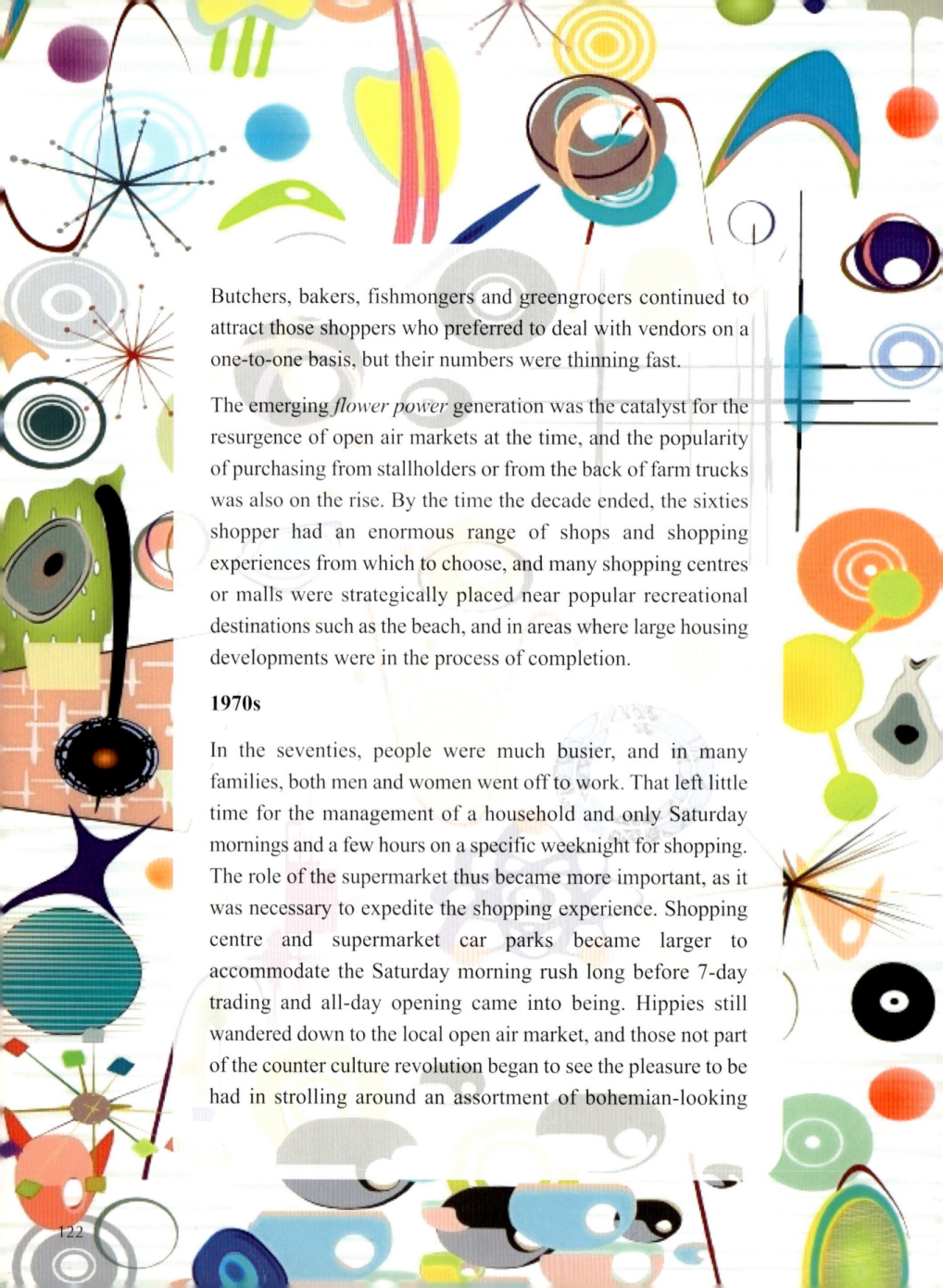

Butchers, bakers, fishmongers and greengrocers continued to attract those shoppers who preferred to deal with vendors on a one-to-one basis, but their numbers were thinning fast.

The emerging *flower power* generation was the catalyst for the resurgence of open air markets at the time, and the popularity of purchasing from stallholders or from the back of farm trucks was also on the rise. By the time the decade ended, the sixties shopper had an enormous range of shops and shopping experiences from which to choose, and many shopping centres or malls were strategically placed near popular recreational destinations such as the beach, and in areas where large housing developments were in the process of completion.

1970s

In the seventies, people were much busier, and in many families, both men and women went off to work. That left little time for the management of a household and only Saturday mornings and a few hours on a specific weeknight for shopping. The role of the supermarket thus became more important, as it was necessary to expedite the shopping experience. Shopping centre and supermarket car parks became larger to accommodate the Saturday morning rush long before 7-day trading and all-day opening came into being. Hippies still wandered down to the local open air market, and those not part of the counter culture revolution began to see the pleasure to be had in strolling around an assortment of bohemian-looking

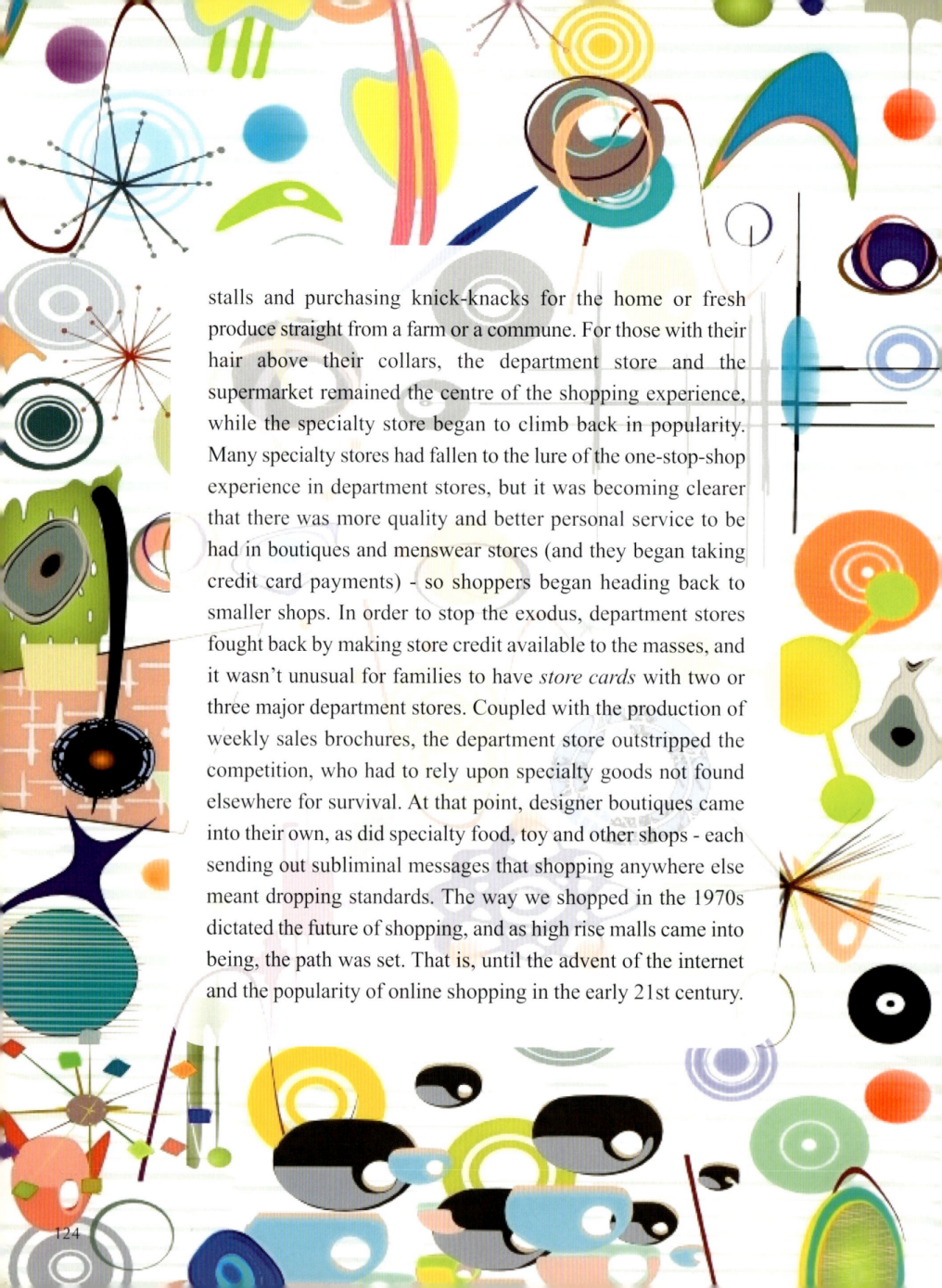

stalls and purchasing knick-knacks for the home or fresh produce straight from a farm or a commune. For those with their hair above their collars, the department store and the supermarket remained the centre of the shopping experience, while the specialty store began to climb back in popularity. Many specialty stores had fallen to the lure of the one-stop-shop experience in department stores, but it was becoming clearer that there was more quality and better personal service to be had in boutiques and menswear stores (and they began taking credit card payments) - so shoppers began heading back to smaller shops. In order to stop the exodus, department stores fought back by making store credit available to the masses, and it wasn't unusual for families to have *store cards* with two or three major department stores. Coupled with the production of weekly sales brochures, the department store outstripped the competition, who had to rely upon specialty goods not found elsewhere for survival. At that point, designer boutiques came into their own, as did specialty food, toy and other shops - each sending out subliminal messages that shopping anywhere else meant dropping standards. The way we shopped in the 1970s dictated the future of shopping, and as high rise malls came into being, the path was set. That is, until the advent of the internet and the popularity of online shopping in the early 21st century.

HOMES

1950s

The 1950s heralded an era of hope for most people, although the threat of Communism was a major issue in the news. Politics however couldn't stop the positivity people felt as the economy picked up. With steady work and a comfortable standard of living, it wasn't long before home ownership became a reality for many families, and the building of new homes went into overdrive. Building materials were still very much in short supply at the beginning of the 1950s, and bricks topped the list. As a result, many brick homes built at the beginning of the decade were made from used bricks that came from demolished homes. Many couples and families built their own homes, and cleaning up used bricks was part of the hands on involvement in the process. Others decided that a brand new world deserved a brand new style of house, and many Nordic inspired homes began to grace the average half or quarter-acre blocks of suburbia. Blocks of flats or apartments seemed to spring up overnight during the decade, initially as a means of housing the post war population that began moving to all corners of the globe, and those affected by bombings in the 1940s. Those blocks were built quickly and cheaply and were eyesores, and their purpose was utilitarian and reasonably short lived. For the rest of the world, homes in the 1950s were built in numerous different styles and from a variety of materials. Weatherboard cottages stood alongside fibro-cement structures,

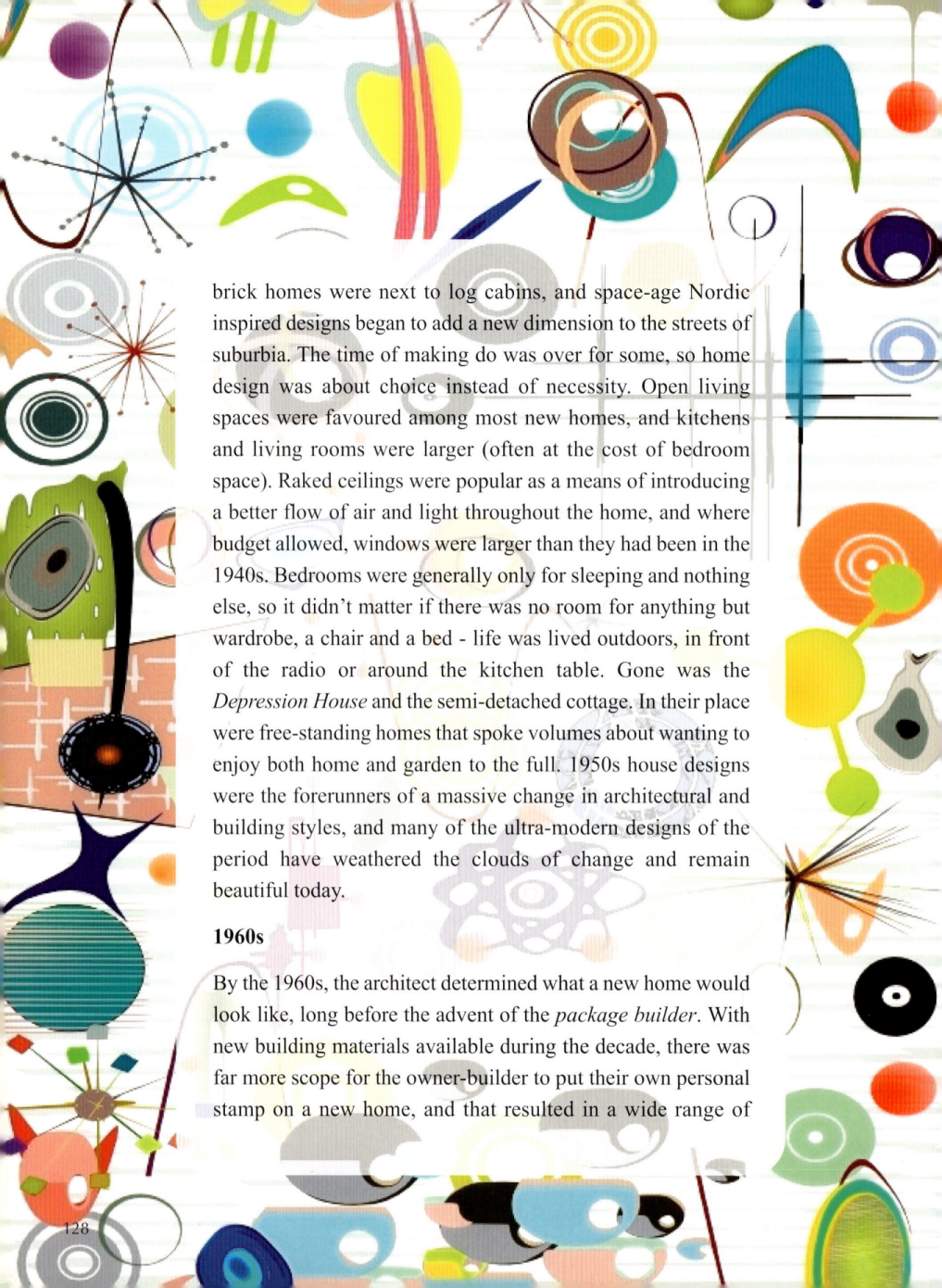

brick homes were next to log cabins, and space-age Nordic inspired designs began to add a new dimension to the streets of suburbia. The time of making do was over for some, so home design was about choice instead of necessity. Open living spaces were favoured among most new homes, and kitchens and living rooms were larger (often at the cost of bedroom space). Raked ceilings were popular as a means of introducing a better flow of air and light throughout the home, and where budget allowed, windows were larger than they had been in the 1940s. Bedrooms were generally only for sleeping and nothing else, so it didn't matter if there was no room for anything but wardrobe, a chair and a bed - life was lived outdoors, in front of the radio or around the kitchen table. Gone was the *Depression House* and the semi-detached cottage. In their place were free-standing homes that spoke volumes about wanting to enjoy both home and garden to the full. 1950s house designs were the forerunners of a massive change in architectural and building styles, and many of the ultra-modern designs of the period have weathered the clouds of change and remain beautiful today.

1960s

By the 1960s, the architect determined what a new home would look like, long before the advent of the *package builder*. With new building materials available during the decade, there was far more scope for the owner-builder to put their own personal stamp on a new home, and that resulted in a wide range of

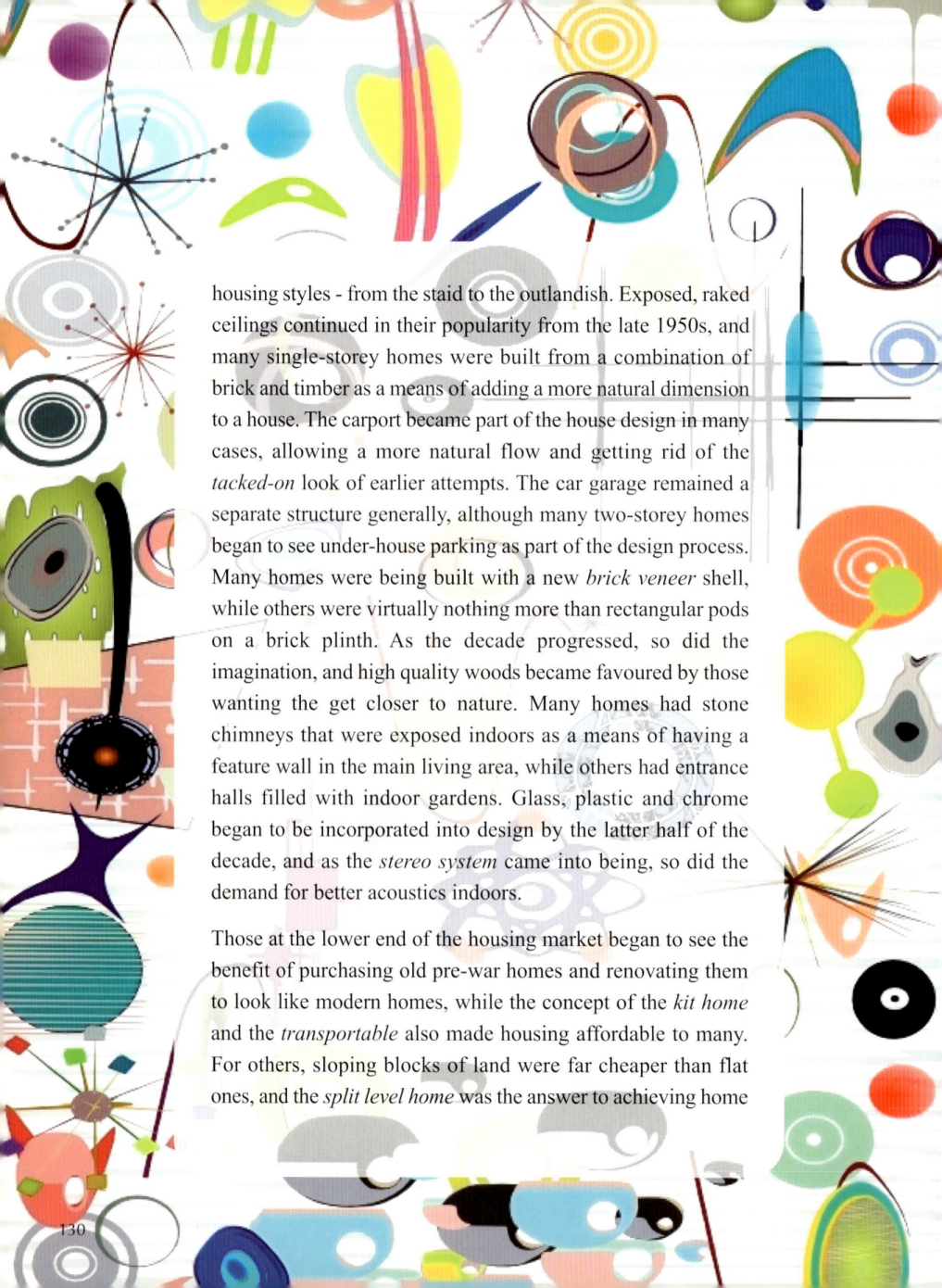

housing styles - from the staid to the outlandish. Exposed, raked ceilings continued in their popularity from the late 1950s, and many single-storey homes were built from a combination of brick and timber as a means of adding a more natural dimension to a house. The carport became part of the house design in many cases, allowing a more natural flow and getting rid of the *tacked-on* look of earlier attempts. The car garage remained a separate structure generally, although many two-storey homes began to see under-house parking as part of the design process. Many homes were being built with a new *brick veneer* shell, while others were virtually nothing more than rectangular pods on a brick plinth. As the decade progressed, so did the imagination, and high quality woods became favoured by those wanting the get closer to nature. Many homes had stone chimneys that were exposed indoors as a means of having a feature wall in the main living area, while others had entrance halls filled with indoor gardens. Glass, plastic and chrome began to be incorporated into design by the latter half of the decade, and as the *stereo system* came into being, so did the demand for better acoustics indoors.

Those at the lower end of the housing market began to see the benefit of purchasing old pre-war homes and renovating them to look like modern homes, while the concept of the *kit home* and the *transportable* also made housing affordable to many. For others, sloping blocks of land were far cheaper than flat ones, and the *split level home* was the answer to achieving home

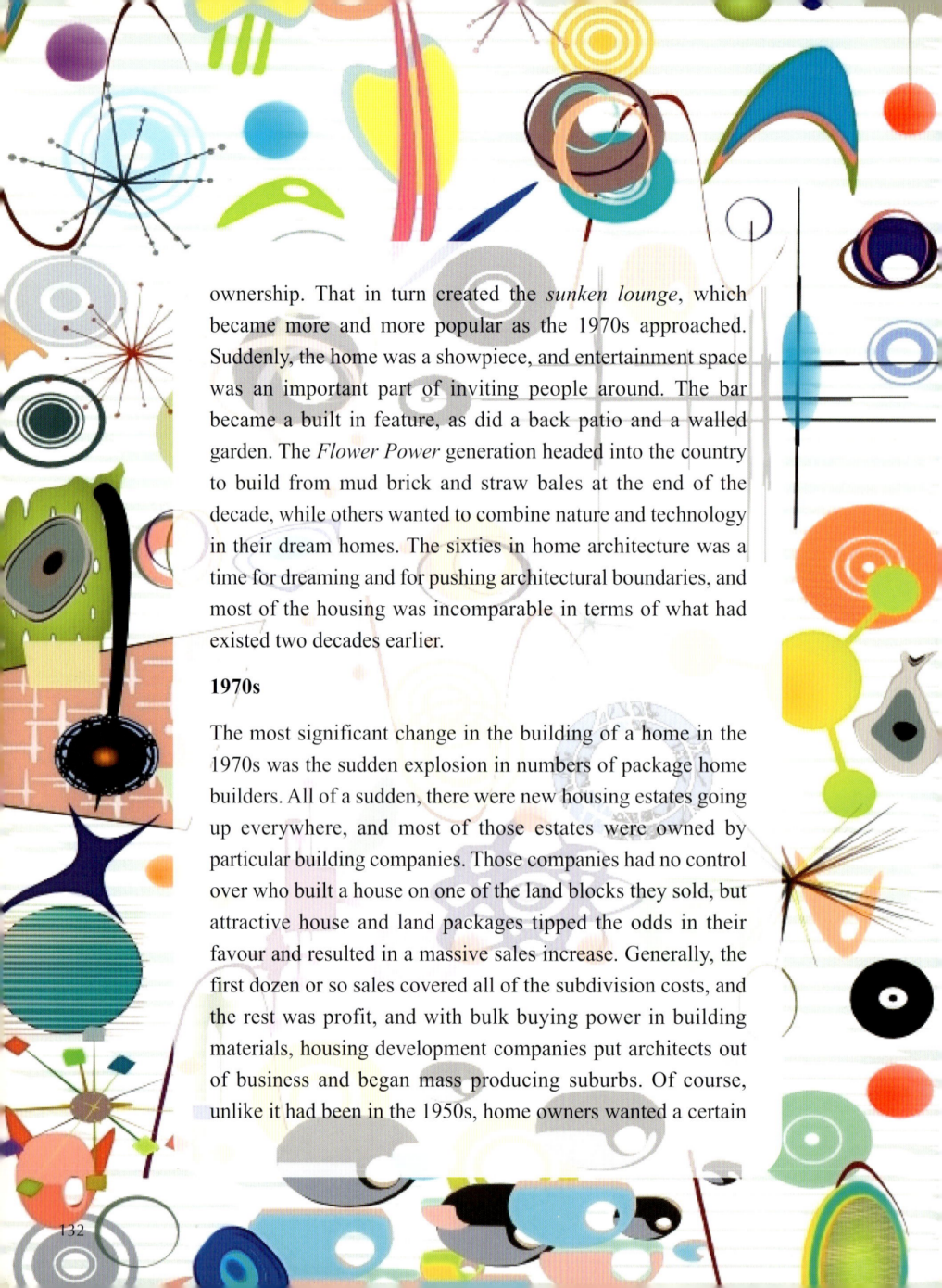

ownership. That in turn created the *sunken lounge*, which became more and more popular as the 1970s approached. Suddenly, the home was a showpiece, and entertainment space was an important part of inviting people around. The bar became a built in feature, as did a back patio and a walled garden. The *Flower Power* generation headed into the country to build from mud brick and straw bales at the end of the decade, while others wanted to combine nature and technology in their dream homes. The sixties in home architecture was a time for dreaming and for pushing architectural boundaries, and most of the housing was incomparable in terms of what had existed two decades earlier.

1970s

The most significant change in the building of a home in the 1970s was the sudden explosion in numbers of package home builders. All of a sudden, there were new housing estates going up everywhere, and most of those estates were owned by particular building companies. Those companies had no control over who built a house on one of the land blocks they sold, but attractive house and land packages tipped the odds in their favour and resulted in a massive sales increase. Generally, the first dozen or so sales covered all of the subdivision costs, and the rest was profit, and with bulk buying power in building materials, housing development companies put architects out of business and began mass producing suburbs. Of course, unlike it had been in the 1950s, home owners wanted a certain

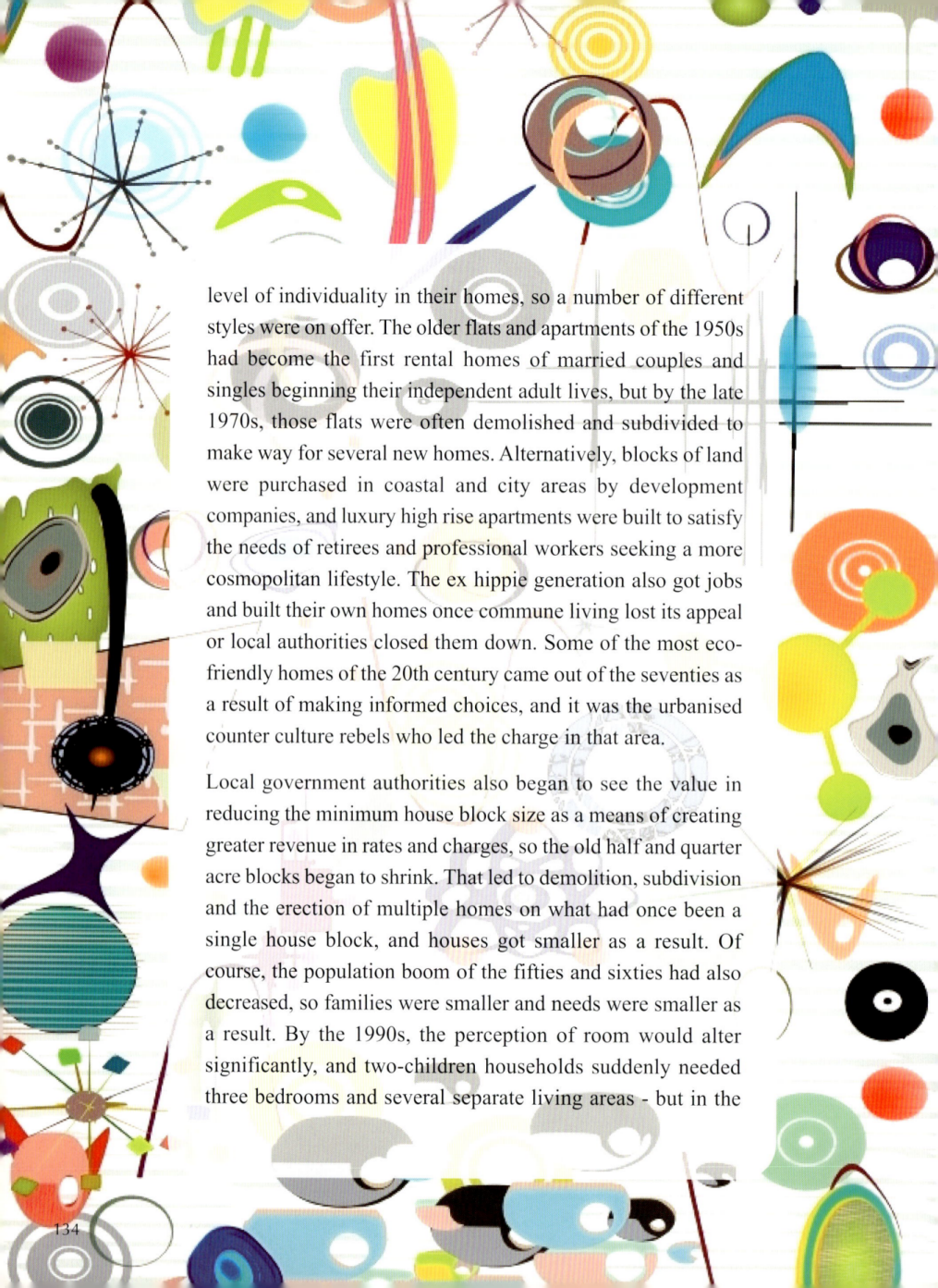

level of individuality in their homes, so a number of different styles were on offer. The older flats and apartments of the 1950s had become the first rental homes of married couples and singles beginning their independent adult lives, but by the late 1970s, those flats were often demolished and subdivided to make way for several new homes. Alternatively, blocks of land were purchased in coastal and city areas by development companies, and luxury high rise apartments were built to satisfy the needs of retirees and professional workers seeking a more cosmopolitan lifestyle. The ex hippie generation also got jobs and built their own homes once commune living lost its appeal or local authorities closed them down. Some of the most eco-friendly homes of the 20th century came out of the seventies as a result of making informed choices, and it was the urbanised counter culture rebels who led the charge in that area.

Local government authorities also began to see the value in reducing the minimum house block size as a means of creating greater revenue in rates and charges, so the old half and quarter acre blocks began to shrink. That led to demolition, subdivision and the erection of multiple homes on what had once been a single house block, and houses got smaller as a result. Of course, the population boom of the fifties and sixties had also decreased, so families were smaller and needs were smaller as a result. By the 1990s, the perception of room would alter significantly, and two-children households suddenly needed three bedrooms and several separate living areas - but in the

1970s, that was still not under consideration. As new building materials continued to increase in popularity and availability, it wasn't unusual to see a street peppered with many different architectural designs in the 1970s, from log cabins and transportables through to double-storey brick dwellings, mock Tudor houses and cement rendered bungalows. The decade of revolution had seeped into most aspects of existence, and the house was not exempt.

INTERIOR DESIGN

KITCHEN 1950s

The 1950s kitchen was the centre of the home, and in many cases, it contained furniture that was built-in instead of freestanding for the first time. No longer the more basic room containing a sink unit and several dressers, cupboards often lined one or two walls, while it wasn't unusual for top end kitchens to have three walls furnished. Pastel colours were big in the 1950s kitchen, and muted colours were generally offset with brightly coloured handles and knobs, as well as a splash of colour at the kitchen window. On the floor, linoleum was the covering of choice - it was easy to mop up spills and it looked so much shinier and newer than floorboards, carpet or cork matting. In the post war years, there was a general feeling of hope, even in light of the wars against Communism being fought in Asia. That hope came into the room where the family

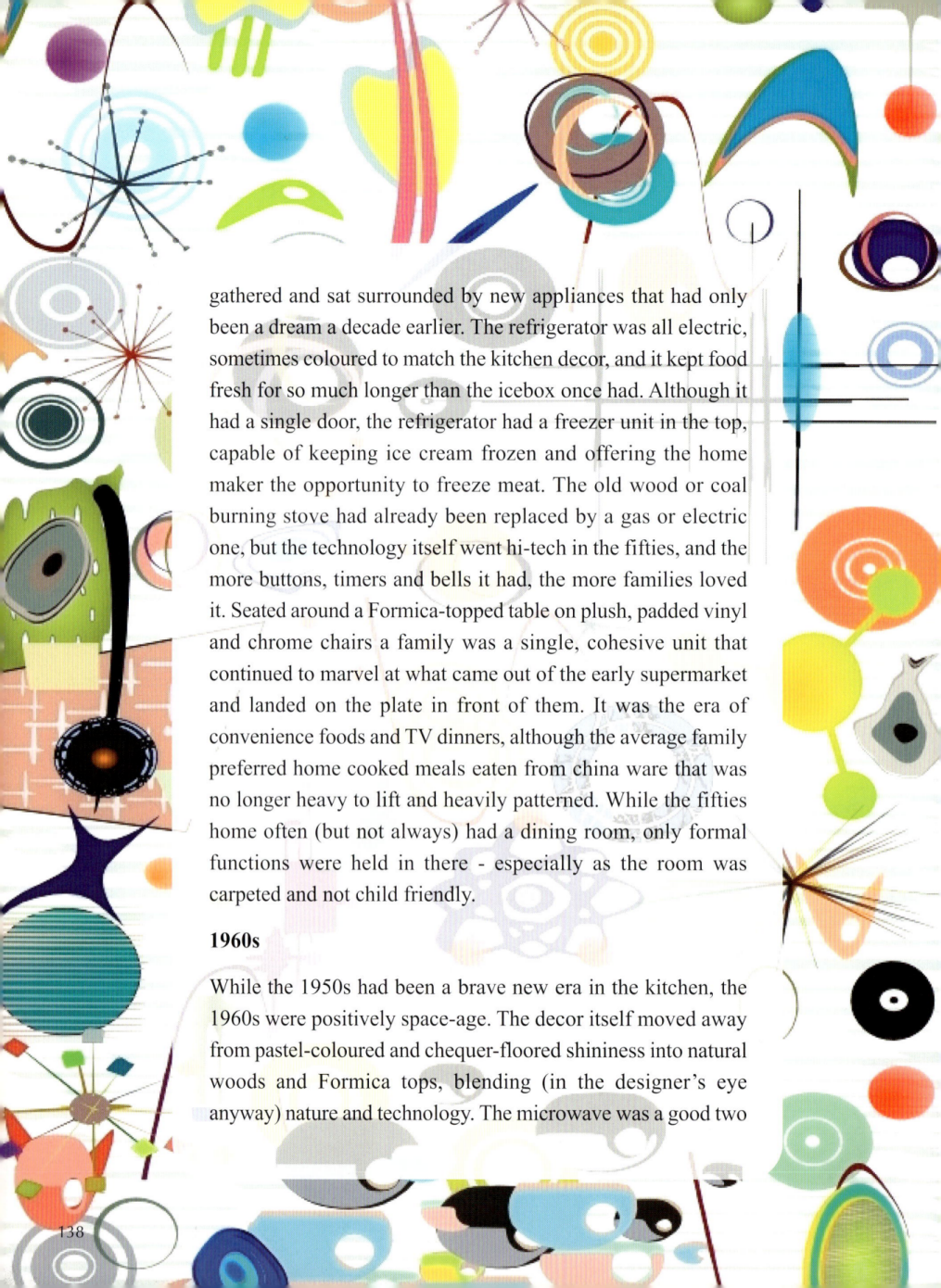

gathered and sat surrounded by new appliances that had only been a dream a decade earlier. The refrigerator was all electric, sometimes coloured to match the kitchen decor, and it kept food fresh for so much longer than the icebox once had. Although it had a single door, the refrigerator had a freezer unit in the top, capable of keeping ice cream frozen and offering the home maker the opportunity to freeze meat. The old wood or coal burning stove had already been replaced by a gas or electric one, but the technology itself went hi-tech in the fifties, and the more buttons, timers and bells it had, the more families loved it. Seated around a Formica-topped table on plush, padded vinyl and chrome chairs a family was a single, cohesive unit that continued to marvel at what came out of the early supermarket and landed on the plate in front of them. It was the era of convenience foods and TV dinners, although the average family preferred home cooked meals eaten from china ware that was no longer heavy to lift and heavily patterned. While the fifties home often (but not always) had a dining room, only formal functions were held in there - especially as the room was carpeted and not child friendly.

1960s

While the 1950s had been a brave new era in the kitchen, the 1960s were positively space-age. The decor itself moved away from pastel-coloured and chequer-floored shininess into natural woods and Formica tops, blending (in the designer's eye anyway) nature and technology. The microwave was a good two

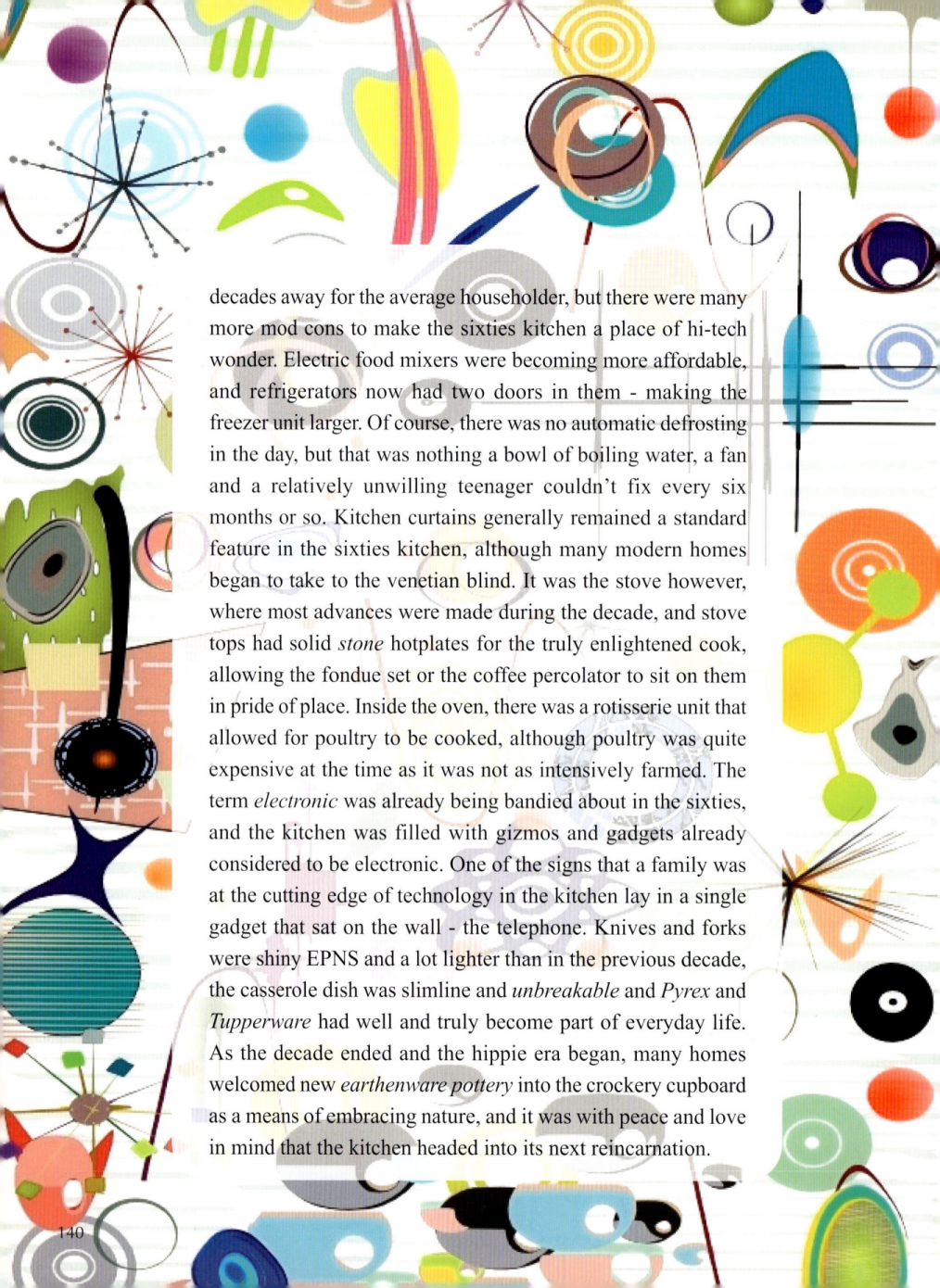

decades away for the average householder, but there were many more mod cons to make the sixties kitchen a place of hi-tech wonder. Electric food mixers were becoming more affordable, and refrigerators now had two doors in them - making the freezer unit larger. Of course, there was no automatic defrosting in the day, but that was nothing a bowl of boiling water, a fan and a relatively unwilling teenager couldn't fix every six months or so. Kitchen curtains generally remained a standard feature in the sixties kitchen, although many modern homes began to take to the venetian blind. It was the stove however, where most advances were made during the decade, and stove tops had solid *stone* hotplates for the truly enlightened cook, allowing the fondue set or the coffee percolator to sit on them in pride of place. Inside the oven, there was a rotisserie unit that allowed for poultry to be cooked, although poultry was quite expensive at the time as it was not as intensively farmed. The term *electronic* was already being bandied about in the sixties, and the kitchen was filled with gizmos and gadgets already considered to be electronic. One of the signs that a family was at the cutting edge of technology in the kitchen lay in a single gadget that sat on the wall - the telephone. Knives and forks were shiny EPNS and a lot lighter than in the previous decade, the casserole dish was slimline and *unbreakable* and *Pyrex* and *Tupperware* had well and truly become part of everyday life. As the decade ended and the hippie era began, many homes welcomed new *earthenware pottery* into the crockery cupboard as a means of embracing nature, and it was with peace and love in mind that the kitchen headed into its next reincarnation.

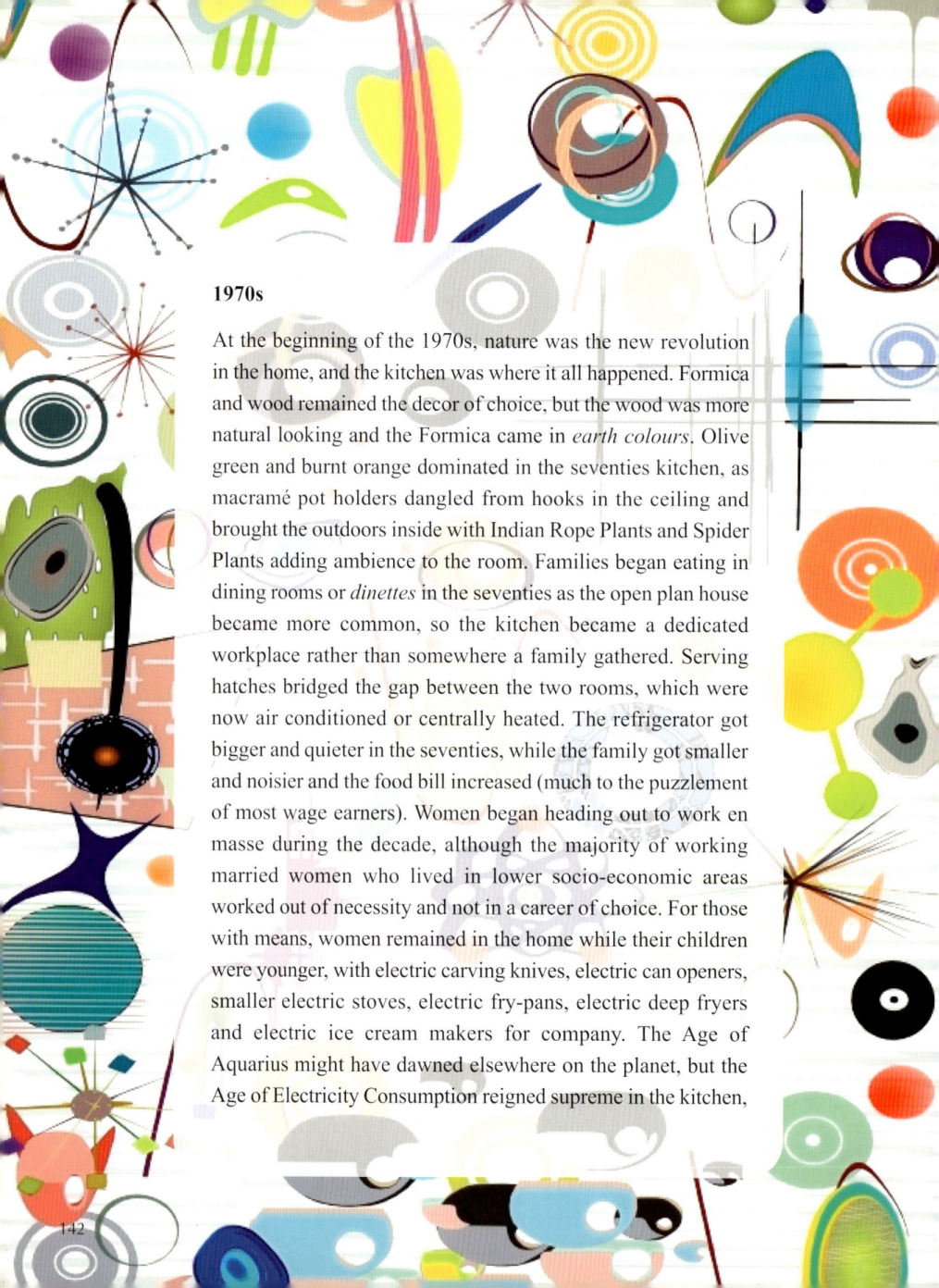

1970s

At the beginning of the 1970s, nature was the new revolution in the home, and the kitchen was where it all happened. Formica and wood remained the decor of choice, but the wood was more natural looking and the Formica came in *earth colours*. Olive green and burnt orange dominated in the seventies kitchen, as macramé pot holders dangled from hooks in the ceiling and brought the outdoors inside with Indian Rope Plants and Spider Plants adding ambience to the room. Families began eating in dining rooms or *dinettes* in the seventies as the open plan house became more common, so the kitchen became a dedicated workplace rather than somewhere a family gathered. Serving hatches bridged the gap between the two rooms, which were now air conditioned or centrally heated. The refrigerator got bigger and quieter in the seventies, while the family got smaller and noisier and the food bill increased (much to the puzzlement of most wage earners). Women began heading out to work en masse during the decade, although the majority of working married women who lived in lower socio-economic areas worked out of necessity and not in a career of choice. For those with means, women remained in the home while their children were younger, with electric carving knives, electric can openers, smaller electric stoves, electric fry-pans, electric deep fryers and electric ice cream makers for company. The Age of Aquarius might have dawned elsewhere on the planet, but the Age of Electricity Consumption reigned supreme in the kitchen,

and as the decade progressed, so did technology that cluttered kitchens with all manner of powered gadgetry.

By the end of the decade, radios and televisions were often part of a kitchen, the first microwaves had been installed by the wealthy and were roasting chickens with the help of yeast extract to create a crispy skin, and many families lived on fried foods. The milkman stopped delivering in many suburbs as the supermarket robbed him of his livelihood, bread would only be eaten by teenagers if it came sliced and in a plastic bag, and the most terrifying appliance of all came into existence - the waste disposal unit! The noisiest, most cantankerous labour-saving device of all was installed in kitchen sinks and magically macerated food scraps, deafening the user and terrifying small children as it sat dragon-like and menacing in a large hole in the sink. The decade of peace and love had finally become the decade of over-manufacturing that resulted in a game of appliance one-up-man-ship that continues today.

LIVING AREAS 1950s

The living room spaces of the 1950s were all about celebrating the comforts available after years of war and rationing. New homes became more spacious and airy, and decor generally matched it. When the family came together in the evening to gather around the radio, they sat on arm chairs with wooden arms and legs and plush upholstery. The sofa was around at the time, and many homes had them, but they weren't the heavy,

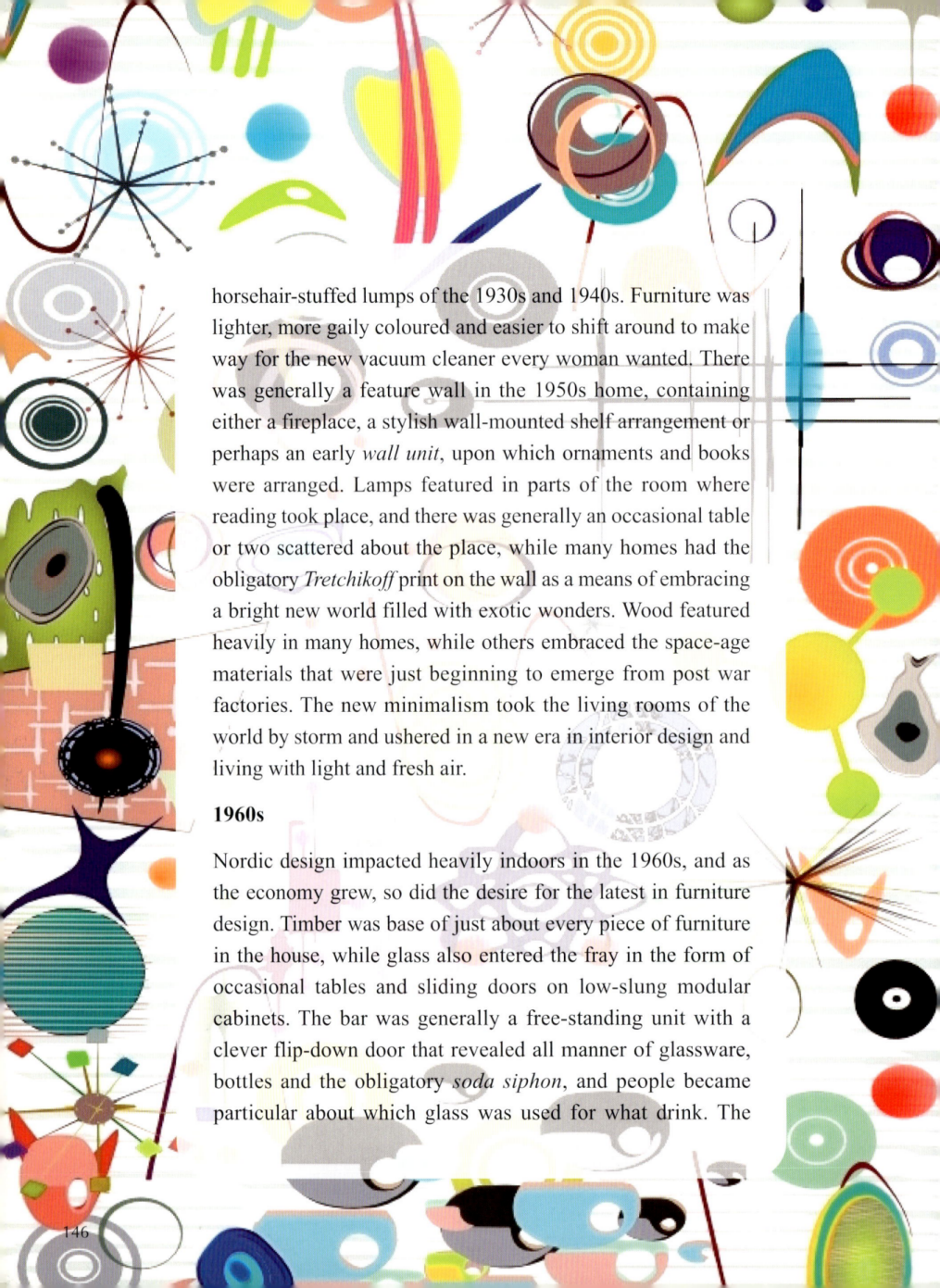

horsehair-stuffed lumps of the 1930s and 1940s. Furniture was lighter, more gaily coloured and easier to shift around to make way for the new vacuum cleaner every woman wanted. There was generally a feature wall in the 1950s home, containing either a fireplace, a stylish wall-mounted shelf arrangement or perhaps an early *wall unit*, upon which ornaments and books were arranged. Lamps featured in parts of the room where reading took place, and there was generally an occasional table or two scattered about the place, while many homes had the obligatory *Tretchikoff* print on the wall as a means of embracing a bright new world filled with exotic wonders. Wood featured heavily in many homes, while others embraced the space-age materials that were just beginning to emerge from post war factories. The new minimalism took the living rooms of the world by storm and ushered in a new era in interior design and living with light and fresh air.

1960s

Nordic design impacted heavily indoors in the 1960s, and as the economy grew, so did the desire for the latest in furniture design. Timber was base of just about every piece of furniture in the house, while glass also entered the fray in the form of occasional tables and sliding doors on low-slung modular cabinets. The bar was generally a free-standing unit with a clever flip-down door that revealed all manner of glassware, bottles and the obligatory *soda siphon*, and people became particular about which glass was used for what drink. The

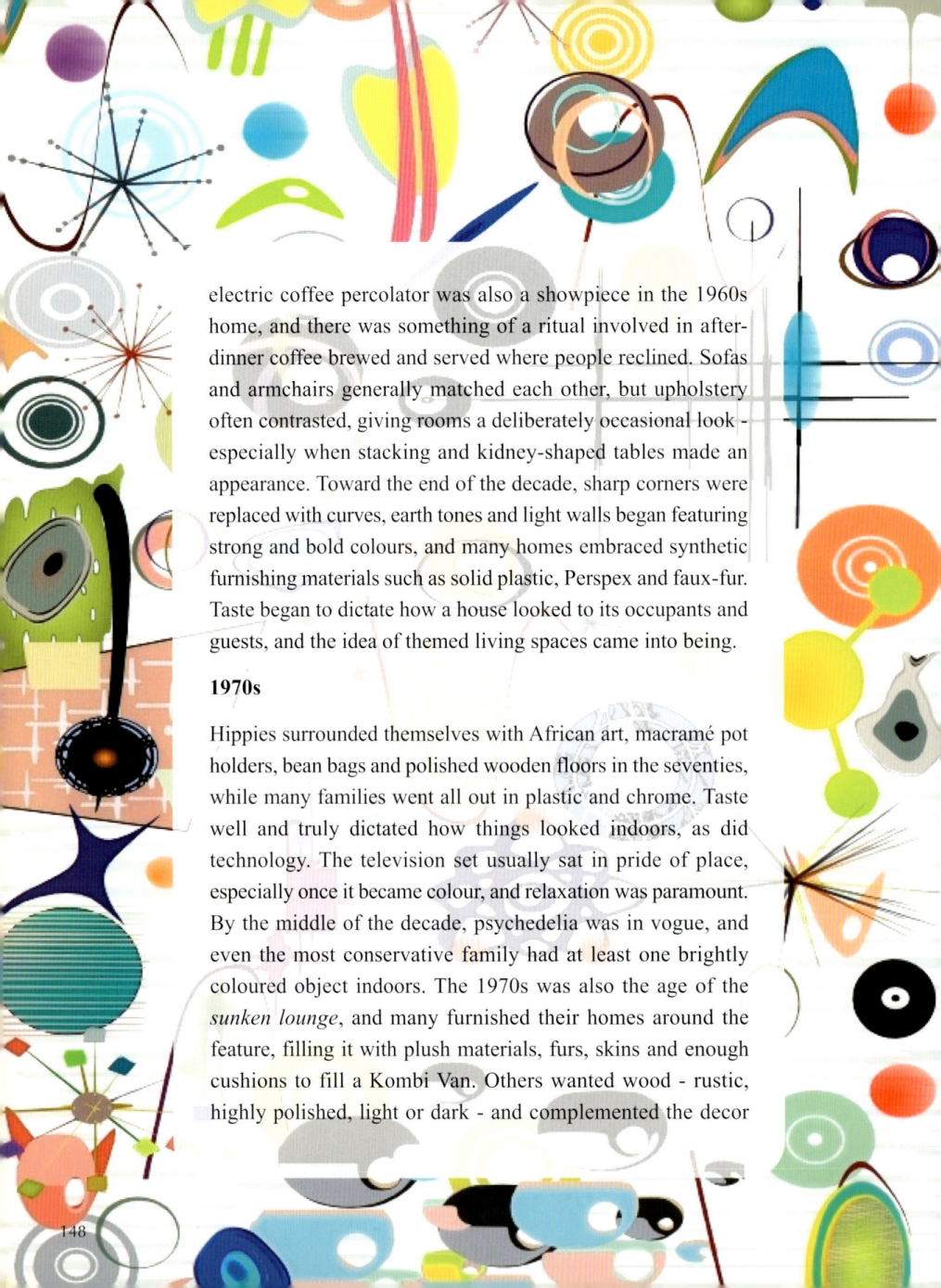

electric coffee percolator was also a showpiece in the 1960s home, and there was something of a ritual involved in after-dinner coffee brewed and served where people reclined. Sofas and armchairs generally matched each other, but upholstery often contrasted, giving rooms a deliberately occasional look - especially when stacking and kidney-shaped tables made an appearance. Toward the end of the decade, sharp corners were replaced with curves, earth tones and light walls began featuring strong and bold colours, and many homes embraced synthetic furnishing materials such as solid plastic, Perspex and faux-fur. Taste began to dictate how a house looked to its occupants and guests, and the idea of themed living spaces came into being.

1970s

Hippies surrounded themselves with African art, macramé pot holders, bean bags and polished wooden floors in the seventies, while many families went all out in plastic and chrome. Taste well and truly dictated how things looked indoors, as did technology. The television set usually sat in pride of place, especially once it became colour, and relaxation was paramount. By the middle of the decade, psychedelia was in vogue, and even the most conservative family had at least one brightly coloured object indoors. The 1970s was also the age of the *sunken lounge*, and many furnished their homes around the feature, filling it with plush materials, furs, skins and enough cushions to fill a Kombi Van. Others wanted wood - rustic, highly polished, light or dark - and complemented the decor

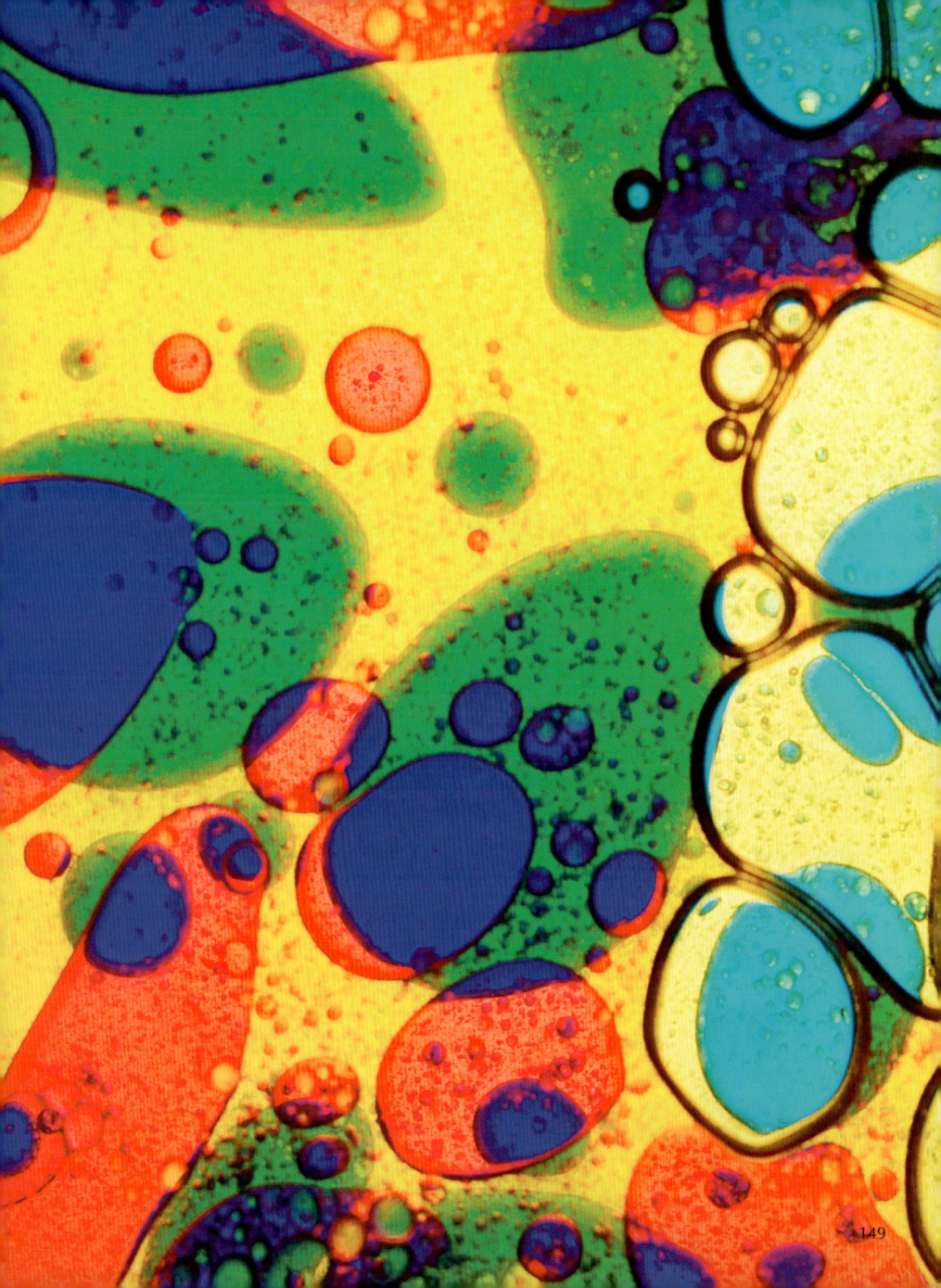

with matching furniture and plants. The indoor plant was important in the 1970s home, as were exposed ceiling timbers and brickwork, shag pile carpet and garishly patterned wallpaper (depending upon taste). Some crammed their homes with an eclectic blend of the best (and the worst) of the decade, while others chose and stuck to a specific theme. Ceiling lights now drooped to within head height and became a feature of their own, and the *Lava Lamp* became a must-have. Indoor aquariums were also popular, and abstract art often hung over where an enormous fish tank sat in pride of place. 1970s decor wasn't about what was available - it was about how householders used what was available to make their own stylish statement about living in the most artistically exciting of the 20th century's decades.

THE LAUNDRY 1950s

One of the busiest days in a woman's life (because it was women who stayed home and raised the children then) was *Wash Day*, and it generally took her an entire day of hard work to take care of the family's laundry needs. The American ads show pictures of smiling families with automatic, front loading washing machines in the fifties, but the average family was a good two decades away from being able to afford such a luxury. Laundry had traditionally been done outdoors until the 1920s, and by the 1940s, most houses had separate outdoor wash houses that included a laundry and an additional outside toilet. Situated next to a clothesline, the wash house became the

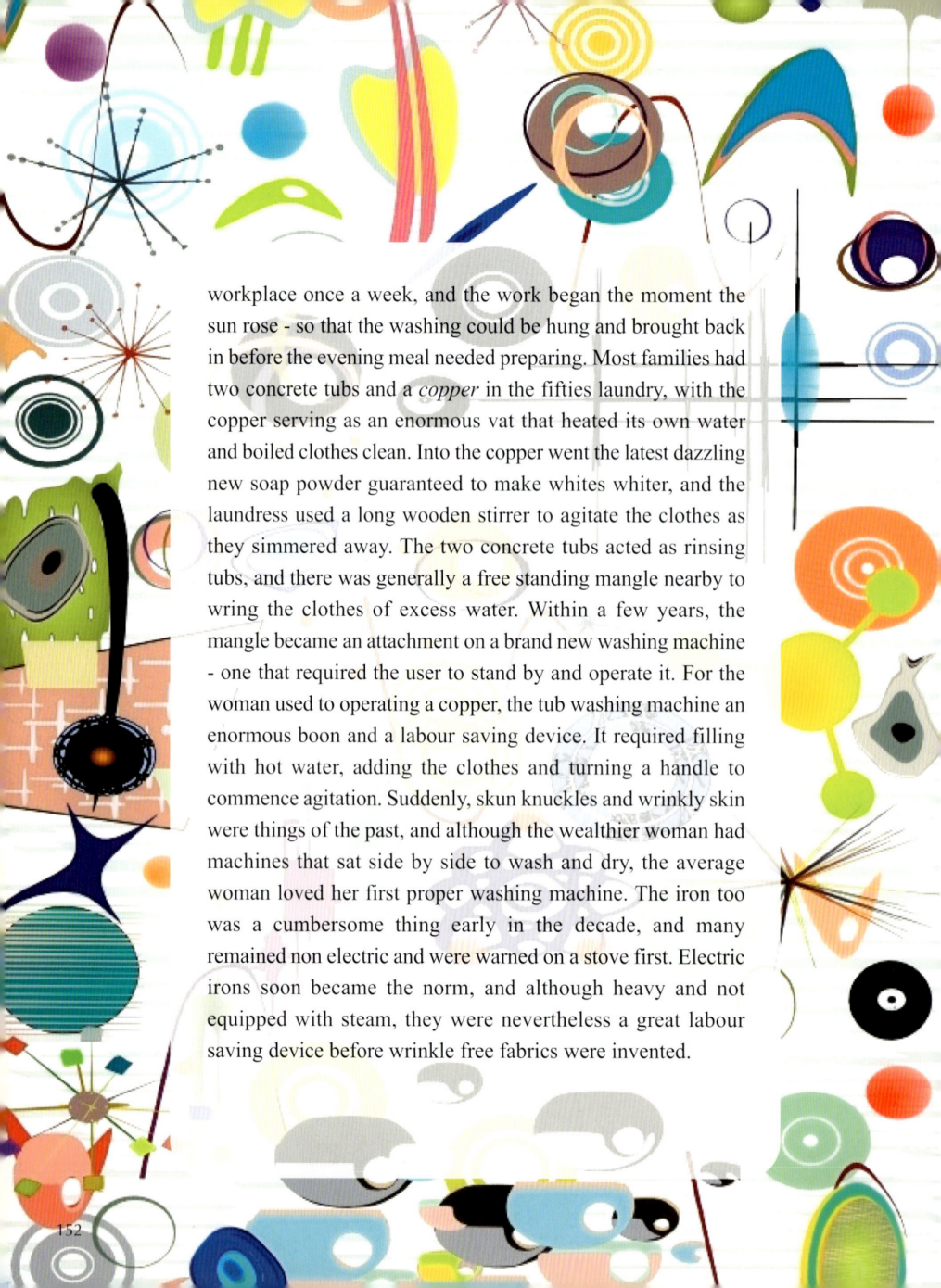

workplace once a week, and the work began the moment the sun rose - so that the washing could be hung and brought back in before the evening meal needed preparing. Most families had two concrete tubs and a *copper* in the fifties laundry, with the copper serving as an enormous vat that heated its own water and boiled clothes clean. Into the copper went the latest dazzling new soap powder guaranteed to make whites whiter, and the laundress used a long wooden stirrer to agitate the clothes as they simmered away. The two concrete tubs acted as rinsing tubs, and there was generally a free standing mangle nearby to wring the clothes of excess water. Within a few years, the mangle became an attachment on a brand new washing machine - one that required the user to stand by and operate it. For the woman used to operating a copper, the tub washing machine an enormous boon and a labour saving device. It required filling with hot water, adding the clothes and turning a handle to commence agitation. Suddenly, skun knuckles and wrinkly skin were things of the past, and although the wealthier woman had machines that sat side by side to wash and dry, the average woman loved her first proper washing machine. The iron too was a cumbersome thing early in the decade, and many remained non electric and were warned on a stove first. Electric irons soon became the norm, and although heavy and not equipped with steam, they were nevertheless a great labour saving device before wrinkle free fabrics were invented.

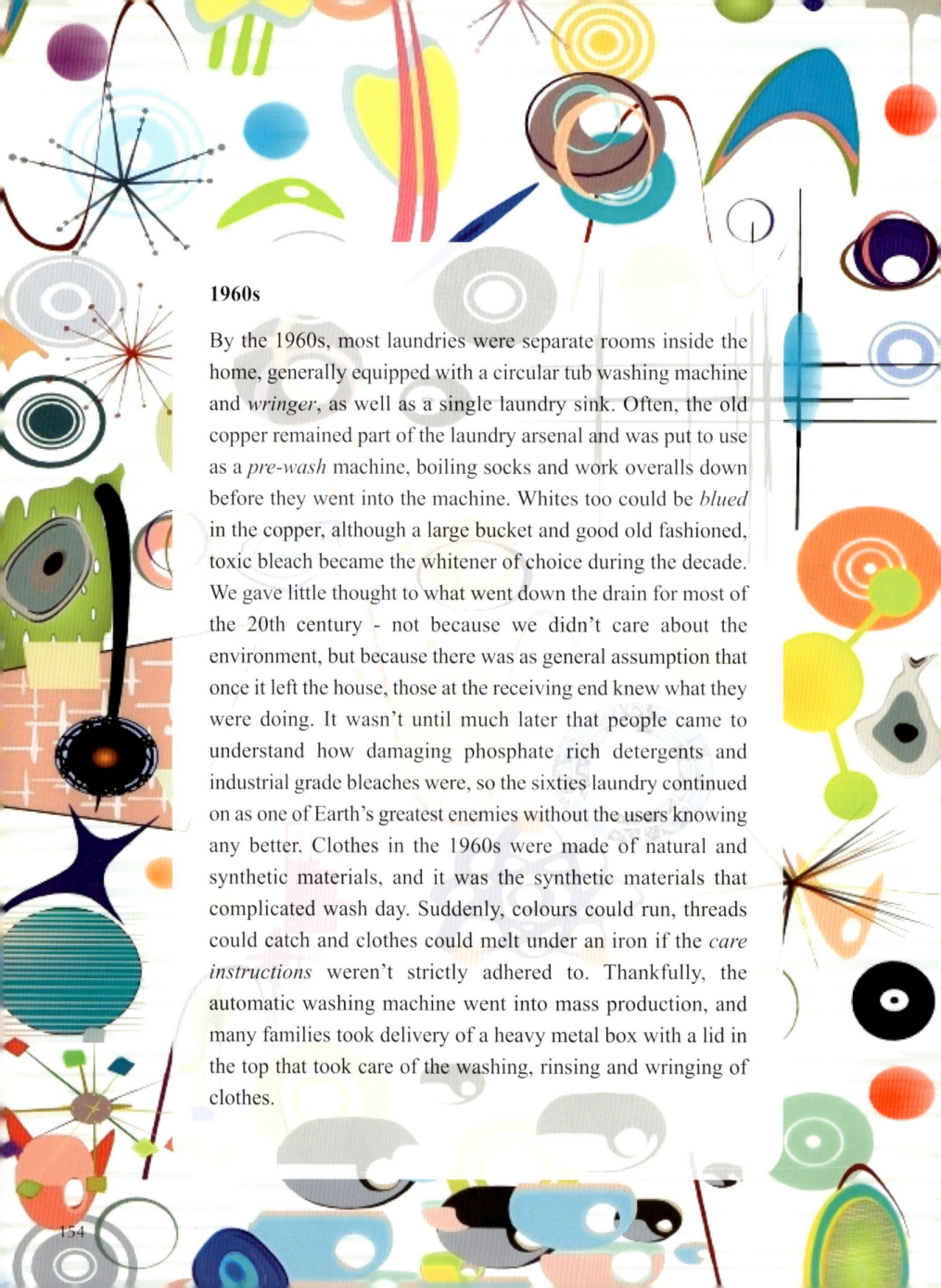

1960s

By the 1960s, most laundries were separate rooms inside the home, generally equipped with a circular tub washing machine and *wringer*, as well as a single laundry sink. Often, the old copper remained part of the laundry arsenal and was put to use as a *pre-wash* machine, boiling socks and work overalls down before they went into the machine. Whites too could be *blued* in the copper, although a large bucket and good old fashioned, toxic bleach became the whitener of choice during the decade. We gave little thought to what went down the drain for most of the 20th century - not because we didn't care about the environment, but because there was as general assumption that once it left the house, those at the receiving end knew what they were doing. It wasn't until much later that people came to understand how damaging phosphate rich detergents and industrial grade bleaches were, so the sixties laundry continued on as one of Earth's greatest enemies without the users knowing any better. Clothes in the 1960s were made of natural and synthetic materials, and it was the synthetic materials that complicated wash day. Suddenly, colours could run, threads could catch and clothes could melt under an iron if the *care instructions* weren't strictly adhered to. Thankfully, the automatic washing machine went into mass production, and many families took delivery of a heavy metal box with a lid in the top that took care of the washing, rinsing and wringing of clothes.

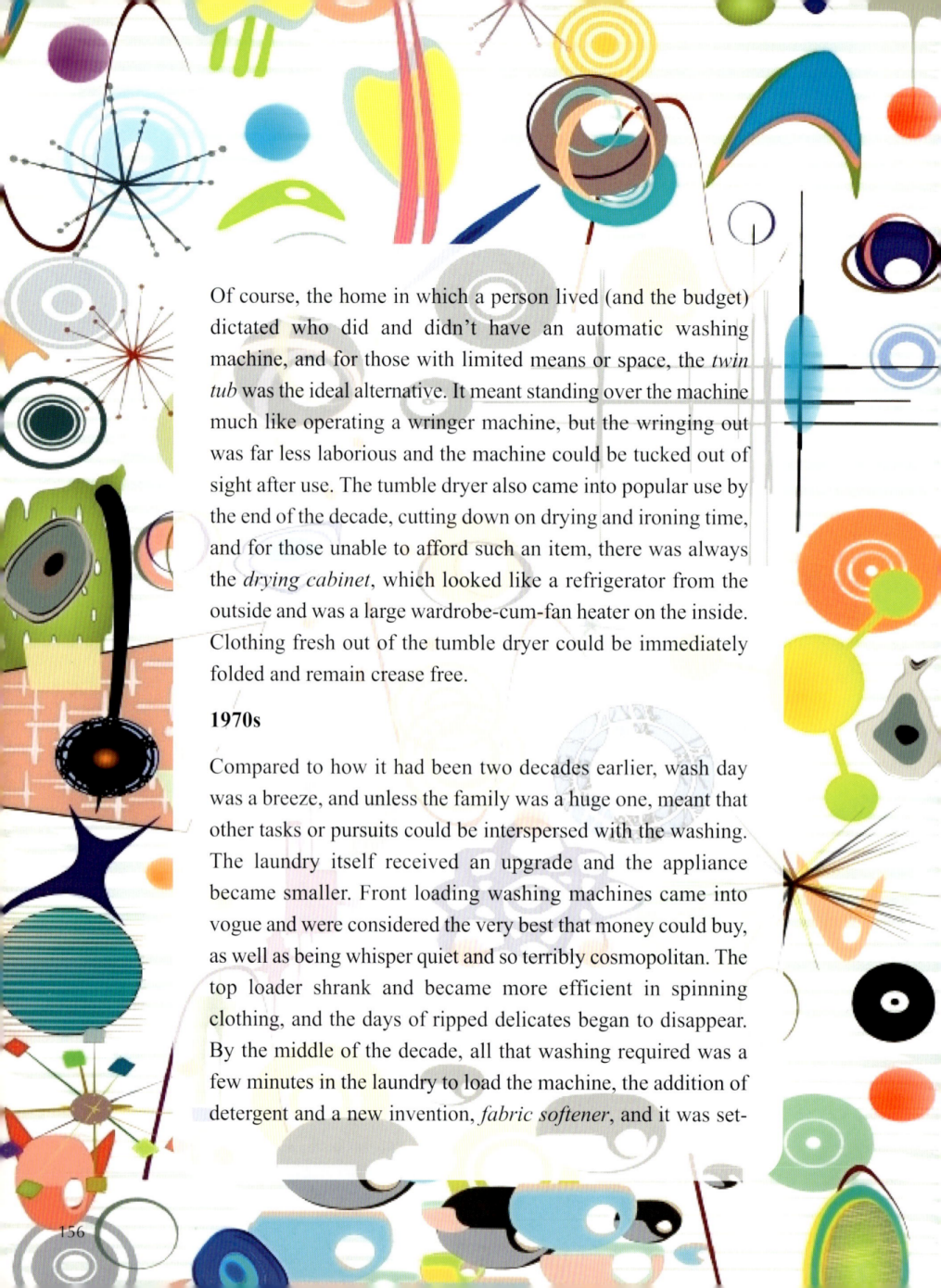

Of course, the home in which a person lived (and the budget) dictated who did and didn't have an automatic washing machine, and for those with limited means or space, the *twin tub* was the ideal alternative. It meant standing over the machine much like operating a wringer machine, but the wringing out was far less laborious and the machine could be tucked out of sight after use. The tumble dryer also came into popular use by the end of the decade, cutting down on drying and ironing time, and for those unable to afford such an item, there was always the *drying cabinet*, which looked like a refrigerator from the outside and was a large wardrobe-cum-fan heater on the inside. Clothing fresh out of the tumble dryer could be immediately folded and remain crease free.

1970s

Compared to how it had been two decades earlier, wash day was a breeze, and unless the family was a huge one, meant that other tasks or pursuits could be interspersed with the washing. The laundry itself received an upgrade and the appliance became smaller. Front loading washing machines came into vogue and were considered the very best that money could buy, as well as being whisper quiet and so terribly cosmopolitan. The top loader shrank and became more efficient in spinning clothing, and the days of ripped delicates began to disappear. By the middle of the decade, all that washing required was a few minutes in the laundry to load the machine, the addition of detergent and a new invention, *fabric softener*, and it was set-

and-forget time. In homes with back gardens, washing was still hung out on the rotary clothes line, but many more homes had tumble driers installed. Those tumble driers were power-guzzling monsters that were often wall mounted in homes not designed to accommodate something that resulted in bruised heads. New homes were often built to allow for front loading washers and driers to sit alongside each other under specially designed benched, and ironing boards too were built into clever cupboard arrangements. The steam iron came into popular use, followed by the *steam press*, which was capable of doing exactly what the dry cleaner did but on a smaller scale. By the end of the decade, the concept of a traditional wash day had disappeared for all but the non electric home, freeing women and men to go about their lives unencumbered by heavy physical toil just so that they could wear clean and pressed clothes. It was a liberation of sorts, but the environmental issues remained unknown by the householder and hidden by the detergent manufacturers - that would take another two decades before change came about.

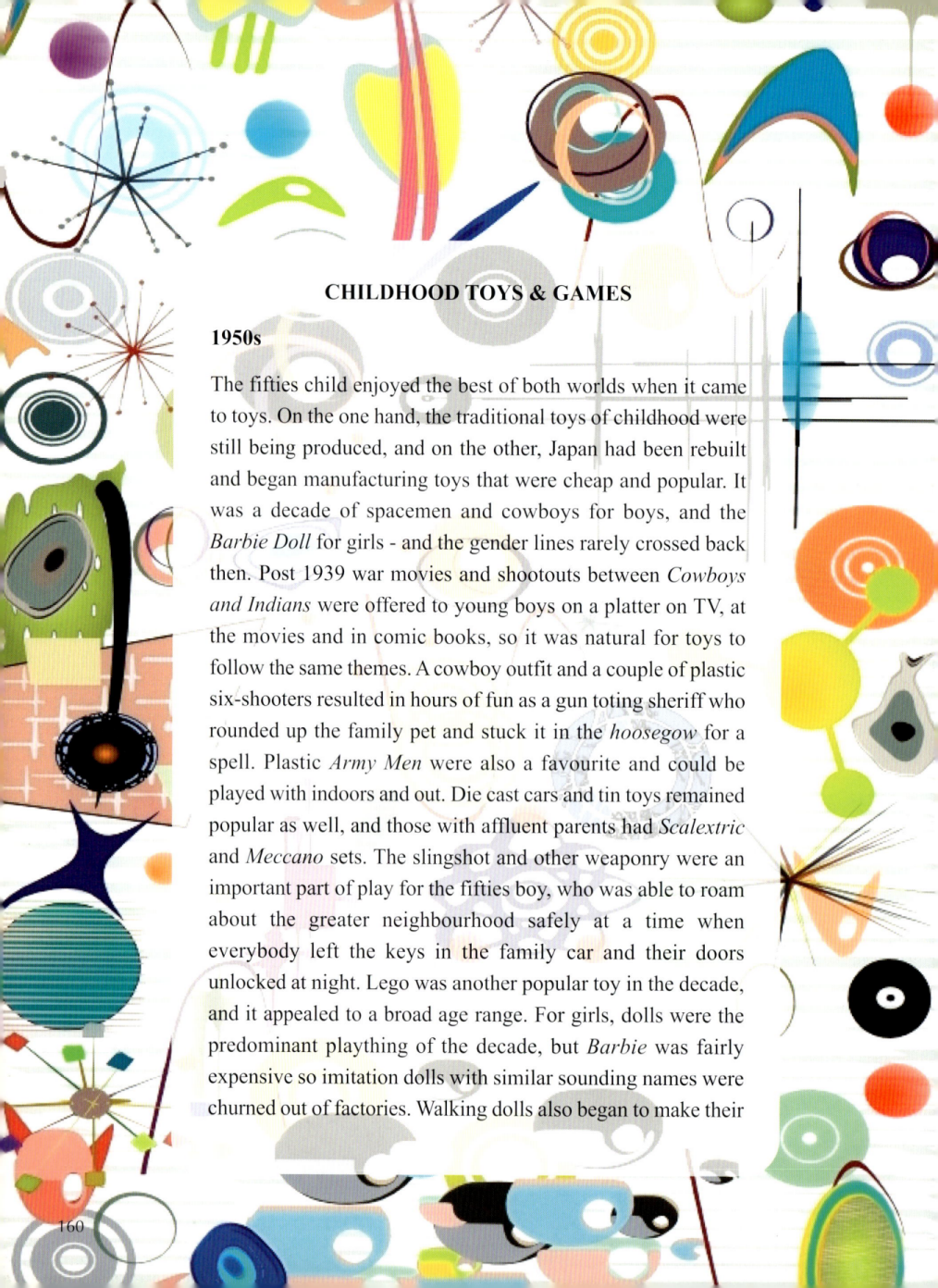

CHILDHOOD TOYS & GAMES

1950s

The fifties child enjoyed the best of both worlds when it came to toys. On the one hand, the traditional toys of childhood were still being produced, and on the other, Japan had been rebuilt and began manufacturing toys that were cheap and popular. It was a decade of spacemen and cowboys for boys, and the *Barbie Doll* for girls - and the gender lines rarely crossed back then. Post 1939 war movies and shootouts between *Cowboys and Indians* were offered to young boys on a platter on TV, at the movies and in comic books, so it was natural for toys to follow the same themes. A cowboy outfit and a couple of plastic six-shooters resulted in hours of fun as a gun toting sheriff who rounded up the family pet and stuck it in the *hoosegow* for a spell. Plastic *Army Men* were also a favourite and could be played with indoors and out. Die cast cars and tin toys remained popular as well, and those with affluent parents had *Scalextric* and *Meccano* sets. The slingshot and other weaponry were an important part of play for the fifties boy, who was able to roam about the greater neighbourhood safely at a time when everybody left the keys in the family car and their doors unlocked at night. Lego was another popular toy in the decade, and it appealed to a broad age range. For girls, dolls were the predominant plaything of the decade, but *Barbie* was fairly expensive so imitation dolls with similar sounding names were churned out of factories. Walking dolls also began to make their

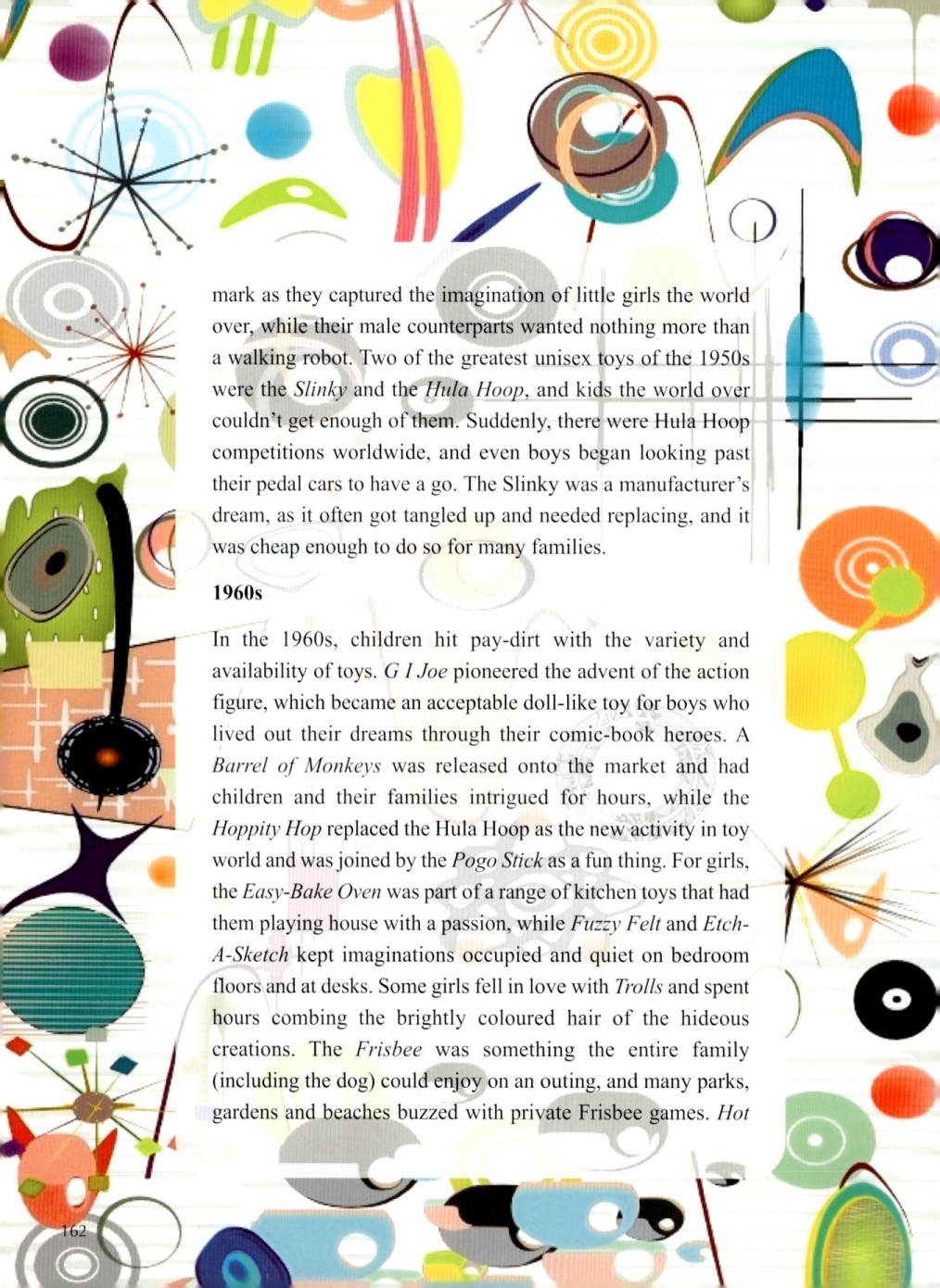

mark as they captured the imagination of little girls the world over, while their male counterparts wanted nothing more than a walking robot. Two of the greatest unisex toys of the 1950s were the *Slinky* and the *Hula Hoop*, and kids the world over couldn't get enough of them. Suddenly, there were Hula Hoop competitions worldwide, and even boys began looking past their pedal cars to have a go. The Slinky was a manufacturer's dream, as it often got tangled up and needed replacing, and it was cheap enough to do so for many families.

1960s

In the 1960s, children hit pay-dirt with the variety and availability of toys. *G I Joe* pioneered the advent of the action figure, which became an acceptable doll-like toy for boys who lived out their dreams through their comic-book heroes. A *Barrel of Monkeys* was released onto the market and had children and their families intrigued for hours, while the *Hoppity Hop* replaced the Hula Hoop as the new activity in toy world and was joined by the *Pogo Stick* as a fun thing. For girls, the *Easy-Bake Oven* was part of a range of kitchen toys that had them playing house with a passion, while *Fuzzy Felt* and *Etch-A-Sketch* kept imaginations occupied and quiet on bedroom floors and at desks. Some girls fell in love with *Trolls* and spent hours combing the brightly coloured hair of the hideous creations. The *Frisbee* was something the entire family (including the dog) could enjoy on an outing, and many parks, gardens and beaches buzzed with private Frisbee games. *Hot*

Wheels thrilled boys of all ages when it revealed the fun to be had in building tracks and releasing cars from up on high, while the more responsible child was let loose on a real train set and the smell of ozone tantalising the nostrils.

Board games became incredibly popular in the sixties, and these included *Monopoly, Scrabble* and *Memory Game*. More fun for the family came in the form of *Mouse Trap, Pick-up Sticks* and *Ker Plunk*, but it was *Twister* and the *Slip 'N Slide* that had the entire family screeching with laughter. Some children played with yo-yos, others tried to put *Mr. Potato Head* together, and the littlies had hours of fun with *Play-Doh* and the marvels produced by *Fisher-Price*. As *Tonka Trucks* and *Matchbox Cars* filled the imaginations of some, others preferred to play marbles, throw a *Nerf Ball* around indoors or dream of the time they could own a remote controlled car.

1970s

It was definitely a boy's world in the 1970s in terms of toys, although girls had their say when the unisex games and toys came out. For the girls, the Trolls of the sixties continued in popularity early in the decade, and Barbie was a stalwart who never aged and got herself a boyfriend and a more independent life. A newcomer to the female toy market was *Holly Hobbie*, who went from being a mere toy to a decorating phenomenon for women of all ages, but it was the *Cabbage Patch Doll* that set the world on fire and began an obsession that became a

multi-million dollar winner at the tills. For the boys however, the new age super hero was upon them, and *Action Jackson* vied for top spot against *Stretch Armstrong* and the *Six Million Dollar Man*. A need for speed was satisfied with remote controlled cars becoming more available within the family budget, and *Evel Knievel* was the ultimate in speed heroes. In childhood, as it was in adulthood, the times were changing, and many toys began crossing the great gender divide. Girls and boys alike fell in love with *Star Wars* and the *Rubik's Cube.* As *Smurfs* came into being, so did a massive merchandising success, but the most massive of all came later in the decade and changed the face of childhood play forever - the *Atari*. Almost immediately, the ant farms, kites, *Sno-Cone* machines and many other timeless favourites fell by the wayside and the age of the computer game began. Soon, children would leave the simple pleasures of shooting at the family pet with a cap gun and head indoors to shoot electronic ducks or battle it out on electronic racetracks. The age of peace and reason was over - the age of space exploration and electronic wizardry had arrived, and it was only going to grow beyond anybody's expectations.

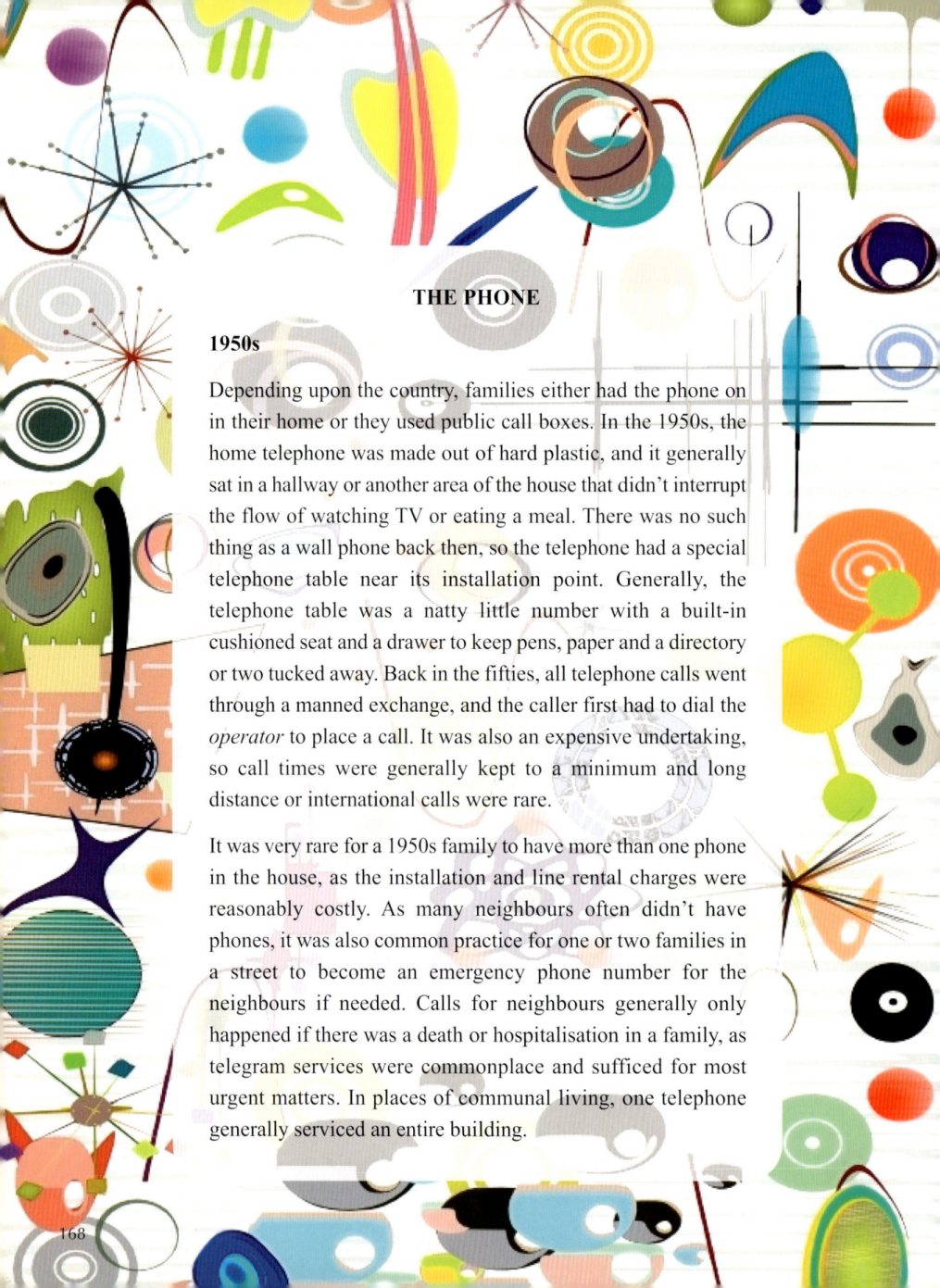

THE PHONE

1950s

Depending upon the country, families either had the phone on in their home or they used public call boxes. In the 1950s, the home telephone was made out of hard plastic, and it generally sat in a hallway or another area of the house that didn't interrupt the flow of watching TV or eating a meal. There was no such thing as a wall phone back then, so the telephone had a special telephone table near its installation point. Generally, the telephone table was a natty little number with a built-in cushioned seat and a drawer to keep pens, paper and a directory or two tucked away. Back in the fifties, all telephone calls went through a manned exchange, and the caller first had to dial the *operator* to place a call. It was also an expensive undertaking, so call times were generally kept to a minimum and long distance or international calls were rare.

It was very rare for a 1950s family to have more than one phone in the house, as the installation and line rental charges were reasonably costly. As many neighbours often didn't have phones, it was also common practice for one or two families in a street to become an emergency phone number for the neighbours if needed. Calls for neighbours generally only happened if there was a death or hospitalisation in a family, as telegram services were commonplace and sufficed for most urgent matters. In places of communal living, one telephone generally serviced an entire building.

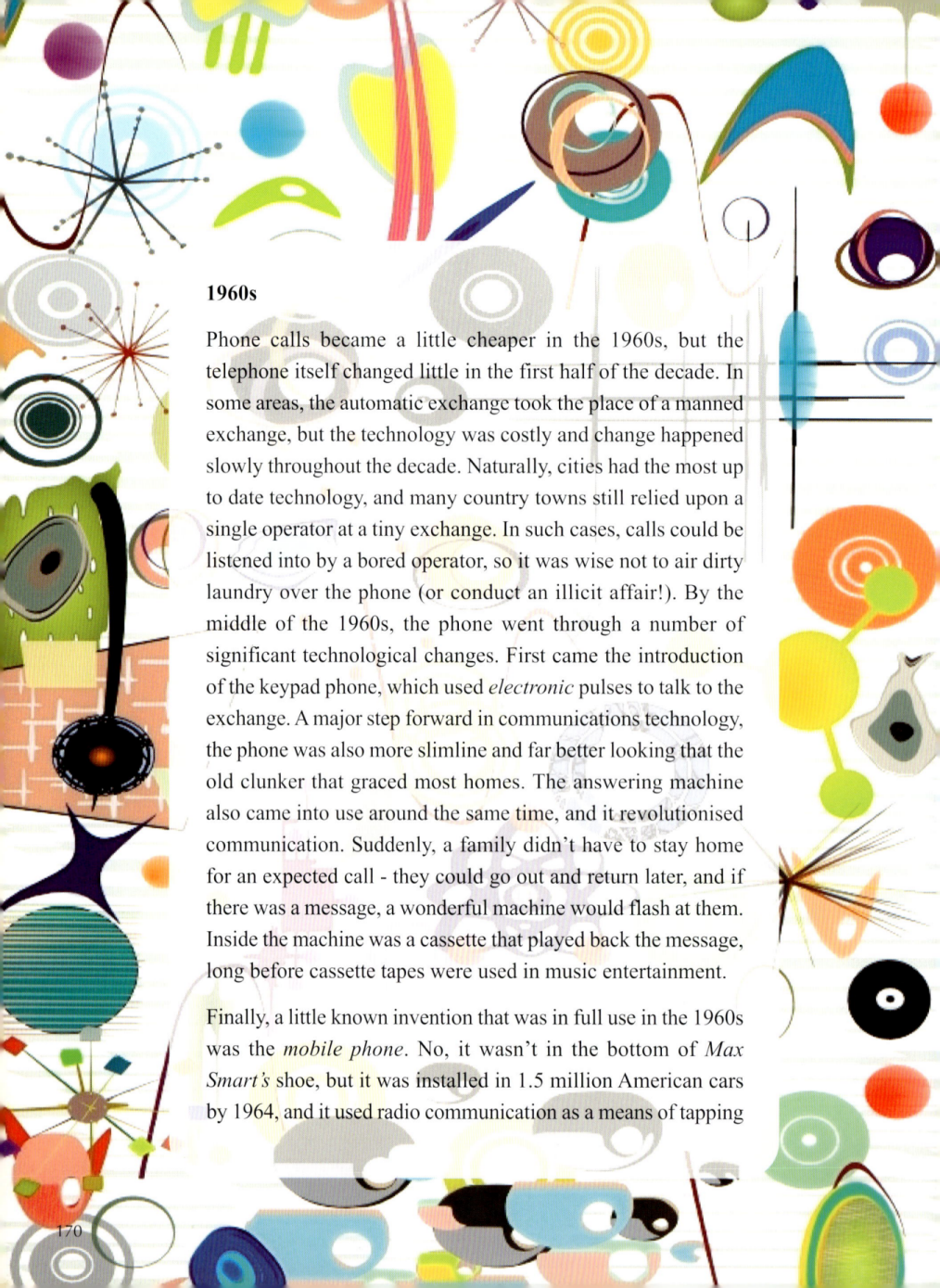

1960s

Phone calls became a little cheaper in the 1960s, but the telephone itself changed little in the first half of the decade. In some areas, the automatic exchange took the place of a manned exchange, but the technology was costly and change happened slowly throughout the decade. Naturally, cities had the most up to date technology, and many country towns still relied upon a single operator at a tiny exchange. In such cases, calls could be listened into by a bored operator, so it was wise not to air dirty laundry over the phone (or conduct an illicit affair!). By the middle of the 1960s, the phone went through a number of significant technological changes. First came the introduction of the keypad phone, which used *electronic* pulses to talk to the exchange. A major step forward in communications technology, the phone was also more slimline and far better looking that the old clunker that graced most homes. The answering machine also came into use around the same time, and it revolutionised communication. Suddenly, a family didn't have to stay home for an expected call - they could go out and return later, and if there was a message, a wonderful machine would flash at them. Inside the machine was a cassette that played back the message, long before cassette tapes were used in music entertainment.

Finally, a little known invention that was in full use in the 1960s was the *mobile phone*. No, it wasn't in the bottom of *Max Smart's* shoe, but it was installed in 1.5 million American cars by 1964, and it used radio communication as a means of tapping

into the telephone system. Generally not available outside of the USA during the decade, mobile or car phones came into greater use around the world during the 1970s.

1970s

By the 1970s, the old rotary dial phone was beginning to become a rare beast, and most phones in homes were push button phones. Not only was the phone lighter and easier to operate, but it was often wall mounted and took up far less space than the old telephone table. The touch phone also had re-dial and auto-dial features, and it came in a range of hip, fab and groovy colours. Soon, phones came in different shapes and sizes and could be matched to decor or satisfy a liking for certain popular character - such as a Disney character (remember the *Mickey Mouse Phone*?)

Phones also went cordless in the seventies, at around the same time that the exchange technology made international and long distance calling much easier. It was still reasonably expensive to make such a call, but the upgrade to old systems made it efficient - especially for business. There was one more sensational advance made in telephone technology in the 1970s, and it happened earlier in the decade. With early mobile phones limited to motor vehicles and operating through a radio system, Motorola invented the hand held mobile phone in 1973. It was 23 centimetres long and weighed over a kilogram, 10 hours were required to recharge it and there was only 30 minutes of